GEAR UP IS FOR ENTREPRENEURS AND
LEADERS WHO WANT TO BRING A NEW
BUSINESS OPPORTUNITY TO LIFE OR
SHARPEN AN EXISTING BUSINESS.

GEAR UP WILL HELP YOU CREATE NEW
MARKETS OR DISRUPT EXISTING ONES.

© 2014 GEAR UP VENTURES AB

Registered office
John Wiley and Sons Ltd, The Atrium, Southern Gate, Chichester,
West Sussex, PO19 8SQ, United Kingdom

For details of our global editorial offices, for customer services and for
information about how to apply for permission to reuse the copyright
material in this book please see our website at www.wiley.com.

Wiley publishes in a variety of print and electronic formats and by
print-on-demand. Some material included with standard print versions
of this book may not be included in e-books or in print-on-demand.
If this book refers to media such as a CD or DVD that is not included
in the version you purchased, you may download this material at
http://booksupport.wiley.com. For more information about Wiley products,
visit www.wiley.com.

Library of Congress Cataloging-in-Publication Data is available.
A catalogue record for this book is available from the British Library.

ISBN 978-0-857-08562-7 (paperback) ISBN 978-0-857-08564-1 (ebk)
ISBN 978-0-857-08565-8 (ebk) ISBN 978-0-857-08563-4 (ebk)
ISBN 978-0-857-08566-5 (ebk)

Set in 11/17pt Berthold Akzidenz Grotesk by
Annette Peppis & Associates
Original design by Ulf Öman
Illustrations by Johan Röstwall
Printed in Italy by Printer Trento

MIX
Paper from
responsible sources
FSC® C015829

GEAR UP

TEST YOUR BUSINESS MODEL POTENTIAL AND PLAN YOUR PATH TO SUCCESS

LENA RAMFELT

JONAS KJELLBERG

TOM KOSNIK

HERE IT IS! THE GEAR UP MODEL

SOME COMPANIES SUCCEED, OTHERS FAIL

WHAT MAKES SOME BUSINESS IDEAS FLOURISH WHILE OTHERS WITHER AND DIE? WHAT COMPONENTS SHOULD YOU FOCUS ON WHEN DEFINING A NEW IDEA OR SHARPENING AN EXISTING ONE? WHAT IS THE SINGLE MOST IMPORTANT ELEMENT THAT ABSOLUTELY MUST WORK FOR A BUSINESS TO SUCCEED? (CAREFUL; THAT WAS A TRICK QUESTION!)

If you are planning to pursue a fresh business opportunity or grow an existing one, you may be looking for some answers. Gear Up can help. Use this guide to determine which of several new ideas you are exploring has the greatest potential. You can also use it to decide whether to push ahead with your current business opportunity, or toss it aside and develop something even bigger and better than you first imagined.

Gear Up does not offer solutions to specific problems. Rather, it is a framework for assessing the needs of your particular situation. Your responses to the questions raised in each gear will create an outcome, a strategy, that is unique for you. Think of this book as your personal trainer. It will help you define a training program based on your objectives, but you will need to put in the hours at the gym yourself. It will tell you to do the push-ups, but it will not do them for you. If you stick with it, the payoff for your dedication will be worth it. As you work with the program, you will learn to leverage your most precious possessions: Your relationships, reputation, talent, time, and money.

Gear Up is intended for entrepreneurs in new ventures, and leaders in established organizations large and small around the world, to decide which new ideas are worth pursuing. Once you have chosen your opportunity, Gear Up will help you create a new market or disrupt an existing one. Gear Up is the result of a joint effort between entrepreneurs and academics, and every recommendation in the book has been tested in the trenches by entrepreneurial leaders around the world.

Gear Up is also a valuable resource for undergraduate and graduate students. The academic roots of the Gear Up model can be found in Harvard Business School and Stanford University, and the book is already in use at Stanford and Stockholm School of Economics.

FIRST THERE IS CONFUSION

Tackling a new business opportunity often leads to confusion. You don't know where you're going, the risk seems enormous, and the idea might not even work. You want to test it, but you're not sure if you have the guts and the patience to try, and there are no shortcuts.

THEN THERE IS STRUCTURE

But that's the nature of the beast. As Winston Churchill once said, "Success consists of going from failure to failure without loss of enthusiasm." In fact, many entrepreneurs believe that the first heady rush of plunging into a new venture is the best part of the whole process. So, take heart! Gear Up will guide the development of your business opportunity by helping you create a customer acquisition-centric strategy. As you begin to follow the program, you'll discover that there is indeed a supporting structure amidst the confusion, and your path to success will emerge.

CREATE YOUR BUSINESS OPPORTUNITY

So what are the gears that you're supposed to "gear up" with? There are nine of them, and they represent the most critical components for launching a high-potential company. The gears are Customers, Delight, Customer Acquisition, Business Model, Partners, Competitors, Go Global, Team, and Reality Check. You have to go through all the gears and make sure that they are in sync. If you have done that, and you find that you still have the passion to cure your customers' pain, then you will know that your business opportunity is worth pursuing.

Here's how it works: You need customers—usually a lot of them—and the ones you want to attract are those with a particular "pain" that your product or service can get rid of. For that you need a unique delight, which is some wonderful thing about your product that distinguishes it from your competitors' offerings. But that is not enough! You also need a method of customer acquisition and a sustainable business model. These three gears – delight, customer acquisition, and business model – together make up your sales formula.

As your business begins to grow, you will most likely need to find the right partners. And since you are not launching your venture in a vacuum, you will have to handle competitors who are perhaps tougher, more experienced, and better funded than you are. If your business really takes off, you will go global and take care of customers' pains all over the world. Last—but certainly not least—is your team, which is the linchpin for innovating, delivering, and challenging other companies in all the gears.

People with exceptional talent and the ability to deliver will become the heart of your business, and you won't get anywhere without them. Just make sure you do a reality check once in a while to stay on track.

Ready? Let's gear up! We'll start with the raison d'être for your whole strategy: Customers.

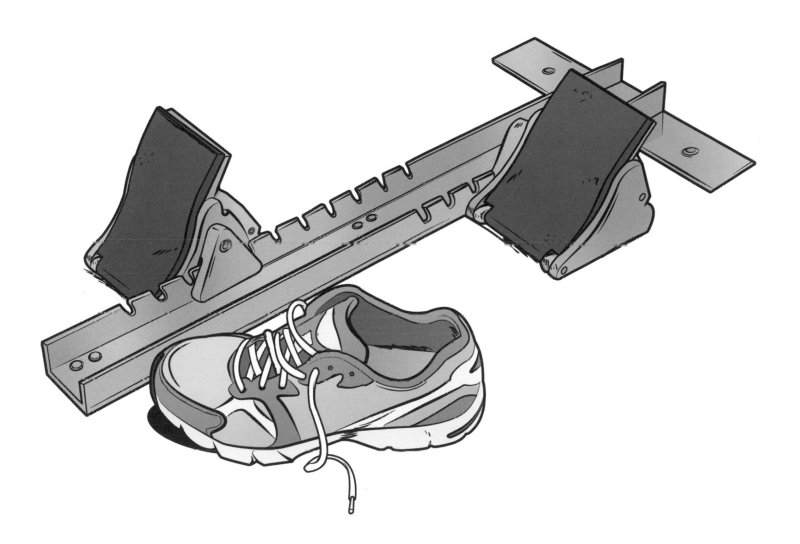

CUSTOMERS

TO CREATE A NEW MARKET OR DISRUPT AN
EXISTING ONE, YOU NEED CUSTOMERS.

CAN'T RIDE WITH THEM, CAN'T SELL TO THEM.

LET'S BE CLEAR: EVERY COMPANY NEEDS CUSTOMERS; YOU WON'T SUCCEED WITHOUT THEM. BUT IF YOU'RE GOING TO WIN THEM OVER, YOU HAVE TO UNDERSTAND WHAT THEY WANT. WHAT IS THEIR UNDERLYING "PAIN"? WHAT PROBLEM OR NEED DO THEY HAVE THAT YOUR COMPANY MIGHT BE ABLE TO SOLVE OR FULFILL? YOU MUST HAVE A PASSION FOR FINDING THE "CURE" THAT WILL EASE THEIR PAIN, AND YOU HAVE TO BE WILLING TO LOOK BEYOND EXISTING OPTIONS TO COME UP WITH THE BEST POSSIBLE SOLUTION.

ARE YOU SOLVING A PROBLEM?

What is your company's "reason for being"? To build a company, you need to solve a problem. The problem doesn't have to be the greatest of challenges, but your company must exist for the clear and simple reason that a group of people out there wants to have the problem solved—and you can solve it. Many times an idea sounds great when discussed in a conference room or presented in a business plan, but in the end it doesn't go anywhere because the product doesn't kill a pain that someone has.

The pain is a problem or issue that bothers the customer. Pain can be expressed as, "I spend too much time doing this," or "I pay too much for that," or "This is too complicated," or even just "This isn't fun!" Your cure, therefore, is what you offer to relieve that pain—how you reduce the time, the cost, the difficulty, or the tedium.

Sometimes the customer and the end user feel different aspects of the pain. (Note that they are not necessarily the same individual. The customer is the person who pays for the product. The end user is the person who actually uses the product.) It is important, therefore, to make sure you have identified them correctly.

HOW WILL YOU KNOW WHAT WORKS FOR YOU AND YOUR COMPANY?

To discover your potential customers' pain, and to find out whether your idea for a new product is a good one, you'll have to step out of your comfort zone—the office. That's right; you will have to walk out of your building and start interacting with your future customers. But how will you know which people to interact with? You won't find them through awkward first points of contact via whatever data

you scrounged up on the Internet. And e-mail blasts of open-ended surveys are simply a waste of your precious time. You could, of course, try the direct approach—simply asking a person what he needs. If you are very lucky, he will tell you. More often, however, your potential customers will have only a vague notion that something isn't right, and they won't be able to articulate what would make them happy. Henry Ford once said, "If I had asked people what they wanted, they would have answered faster horses."

INTERACT WITH YOUR CUSTOMERS!

The best way to identify your potential customers and discover their pain is to observe, participate, and interact with them. Learn how to take notes and draw conclusions. You might be able to deduce that people could be doing something smarter, faster, easier, cheaper, or with more fun. Try it! Go sit on a park bench and just watch potential customers pass by: What are they doing and paying attention to? What gadgets, tools, and equipment are they carrying around? Are they acting alone or in groups? These field trips will reveal important information about your potential customers and their pain. As a Harley-Davidson salesperson once observed, "If you can't ride with them, you can't sell to them."

15

So learn how to ride! Make a prototype, and get out there and sell it! Then get ready to create revised versions; the more feedback you get on different iterations, the faster you'll figure out whether or not there's a pain that your product can cure. Talking to your potential customers and selling them a prototype is far more efficient than spending endless hours in meetings, drawing on a whiteboard and discussing how great your product is going to be. What's more, you will learn a lot about why customers would even consider buying your product—it might not be for the same reason you're selling it! They will give you ideas for improvements, and you will find out quickly what they like and dislike about it. Launch that first version fast!

Apple's design team is still doing it, the designers of Volvo are still doing it, and the founder of IKEA gets a kick out of doing it—interacting with customers, that is. But it is increasingly difficult to persuade potential customers (and end users) to invest time in considering a new product. To start, just getting their attention can be tough. And even once you have that, you'll find that most people already have full schedules; they may not be interested in making a change, moving away from their routine, and doing what you'd prefer them to do instead. There are only 1,440 minutes in a day, and they are already packed with work, travel, meals, exercise, conversations, household chores, entertainment—maybe even a little sleep. Somehow you'll have to convince potential customers that what they've got now isn't good enough, and that it's worth a little time to consider—and with luck, commit to—the amazing alternative that you're offering. Still, while changing your customers' behavior is tough, it can be done. Companies that take on this challenge are usually known as "high risk, high potential."

You don't necessarily have to go that route, however. There are two alternatives to changing customers' behavior. First, try switching up the product. If your customer is already driving a car, why not offer her a different one? Your customer's behavior doesn't change (she is still driving a car), but her product choice does—to yours!

The second option is to offer a product that gives the customer more than she expects. The first cell phones, for example, allowed people to be available and connected 24/7—an amazing breakthrough in communication. But then came smartphones. Now people can not only talk on their phones, but they can also use them for checking e-mail, listening to music, and playing games, no matter where they are or what else they're doing at the time. Now that's added value!

**HOW THE CUSTOMER
DESCRIBED IT**

**HOW THE SALESMAN
SOLD IT**

**HOW THE PROJECT LEADER
UNDERSTOOD IT**

HOW THE FACTORY BUILT IT

HOW THE CUSTOMER WAS BILLED

**WHAT THE CUSTOMER
REALLY NEEDED**

Note! Don't build a car when a bicycle is what your customer really needs.

WHO ARE YOUR CUSTOMERS?

DO THEY SHARE THE SAME PAIN? ADD SHORT DESCRIPTIONS OF THEM IN THE FRAMES BELOW.

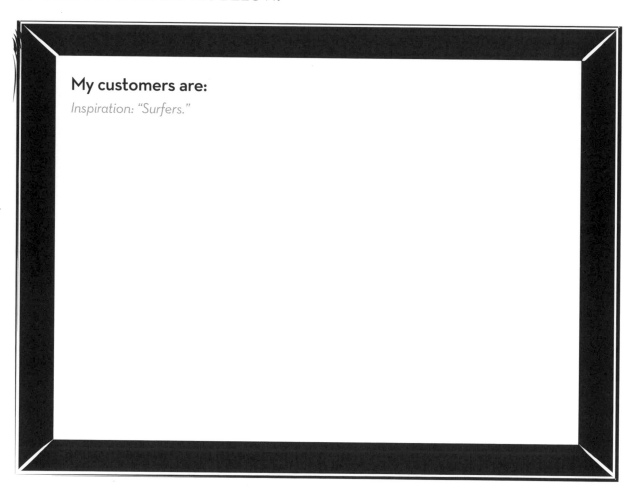

My customers are:

Inspiration: "Surfers."

Note! *How many customer groups do you really have? How do they differ?*

Segment your customers:

Inspiration: Surfers could be divided into smaller segments, such as "Longboarders."	*Inspiration: "Hippies."*	*Inspiration: "Locals."*
Inspiration: "Executives."	*Inspiration: "Surf Pros."*	*Inspiration: "Kids."*

FROM PAIN TO PRODUCT

OK! Now you have a fairly good idea of who your customers are and how their pain can be eased by your product. The next challenge is to communicate that information to your team and create a fully-fledged, marketable solution to your customers' pain.

HERE'S HOW IT USUALLY GOES

You're pretty sure you know what the customer needs; she talks about it and shows you what she wants. She might even have her own ideas about what to do. You and your team listen—and listen well—to translate what you've heard into product specifications. Your team's experience and expertise will influence the layout of the internal project that you design.

The customer's pain has now become a project description. You pass it along to the engineering team, who translates the outline into a road map with milestones and deliverables (engineers are great at this!).

If your team really understands your customers' pain, and your engineers have successfully developed the solution for it, then you finally have a product! And once you have refined the prototype through more interaction with your customers, then you have a product that is ready to launch. Out to the market it goes—usually with a big release party. (The more media coverage, the better!) The sales force then starts looking for leads, while the operations group implements a system for billing, perhaps with an installation fee and a monthly subscription to secure recurrent revenue. And support? Maybe you still need to determine how that will be handled and by whom, and whether to include it in the customer acquisition costs. Still, revenue is pretty good. And the buzz isn't bad, either! Nevertheless, the question lingers: Is it really what the customers want? If they come back for more, then the answer is yes!

OH, THE PAIN!

Do your customers feel pain? What do they say? What have you learned from them? Do you offer a solution for your customers' pain? Do they buy your solution? Is it simple to use? Do you delight your customers? Are you sure? Think again!

WHAT PAIN DO YOU SOLVE?

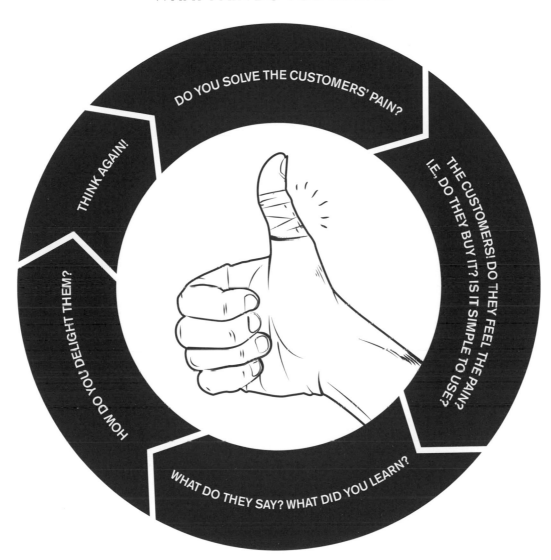

DO YOU SOLVE THE CUSTOMERS' PAIN?

THE CUSTOMERS! DO THEY FEEL THE PAIN? I.E., DO THEY BUY IT? IS IT SIMPLE TO USE?

WHAT DO THEY SAY? WHAT DID YOU LEARN?

HOW DO YOU DELIGHT THEM?

THINK AGAIN!

YOUR CUSTOMERS' PAIN

WHAT PARTICULAR "PAIN" DOES YOUR PRODUCT OR SERVICE GET RID OF?

Explain the pain your customers have:

Inspiration: "It's difficult to see in the dark."

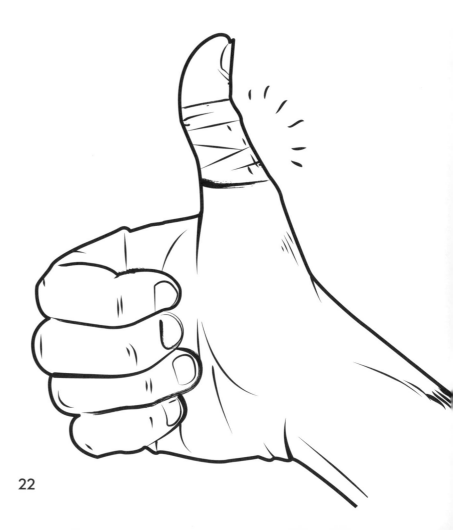

Explain how you cure the pain:

Inspiration: "Lightbulb."

Note! This is hard, but if you can nail their pain and explain how you can cure it, then you are on a roll!

EXERCISE

You are right about your customers' pain because:

Inspiration: "I have interviewed, watched, observed, participated, experienced, talked, sold a beta product, etc."

Would you be able to sell your product on preorders only? Explain why:

Inspiration: "Volkswagen made a prototype of a new Beetle. Strong public reactions and many preorders convinced the company to start manufacturing the car."

CROSSING THE CHASM

You've acquired your first customers—well done! Now what? How do you "cross the chasm," that is, how do you reach beyond your tiny group and move into the huge mass markets? Geoffrey A. Moore developed one of the most influential models for high-potential companies: the Technology Adoption Life Cycle. In his book *Crossing the Chasm*, he explains why most companies never end up capturing mass markets. In a nutshell, it is because they don't realize that different customer groups have different pains. As a result, they fail to turn their "technology" (which is what most high-risk, high-potential companies sell in the early days) into a product that can adapt to the changing demands of different markets. Most companies face some serious challenges when they make the leap to cross the chasm, and even in businesses that do so successfully, no one's really sure just how they did it. But pay attention, because one thing is certain – your company will change!

THE SHIFT

Let's reimagine how a company crossed the chasm many years ago with a product that was intended to save people from the onerous task of getting up off the couch to change the TV channel. You are the head of that company, and you have a terrific, enthusiastic team of engineers.

You assign them the task of developing the product, and they do a great job. The first prototype of your product—the remote control—has eight buttons. The next has 10, and the one after that has 14. You decide it's time to create a design with 20 buttons, but lucky you: the engineers' budget runs out while they're working on the design, and you have to put an end to development. Pre-chasm: Your first customers are thrilled with the new remote because they don't have to budge from the couch anymore, and they love all the fun buttons—even though they might only use three or four of them. Your partners, employees, and potential investors also love it, because they adore new technology!

As the novelty wears off, customers seem to forget why they liked your product in the first place. All they now see is an ugly device with too many buttons to figure out. They toss your creation aside and go back to switching channels the old way. What does this mean? You have crossed the chasm! Your new customers have other demands. You will need to adjust to your evolving customer base and changing market conditions (you might even need to create a Sales and Marketing department!) and find new partners. And you will definitely be rethinking your solution to your customers' pain. Maybe you should check again: Exactly how many buttons do your customers really need?

HOW THE EARLY CUSTOMER DESCRIBED IT   WHAT THE MAJORITY OF CUSTOMERS REALLY WANTED

CROSS THE CHASM

THIS IS YOUR CHALLENGE: TAKING YOUR PRODUCT FROM TARGETING INNOVATORS AND EARLY ADOPTERS TO CROSSING THE CHASM AND TARGETING A MASS MARKET

Your product today

Inspiration: "A remote control with many buttons."

Estimate what needs to be done to cross the chasm

SHOW WHERE ON THE TALC YOUR PRODUCT IS RIGHT NOW >

Your product when "on top"

Inspiration: "An easy-to-use remote control with only one button."

THE CHASM

INNOVATORS

EARLY ADOPTERS

EARLY MAJORITY

LATE MAJORITY

A DAY IN THE LIFE OF YOUR CUSTOMERS

How will they use it?

Inspiration: "A Harley-Davidson is used by a 47-year-old accountant, dressed in black leather and feeling like an outlaw."

Where will they use it?

Inspiration: "On winding roads in the countryside or cruising through small towns having people be afraid of them."

When will they use it?

Inspiration: "Harley-Davidsons are used at the weekend for "freedom rides" when the owner wants to feel alive."

__Note!__ Do you solve different pains in different parts of the customers' user journey? e.g., unpacking, installation, usage, cancellation, etc.

CHAPTER SUMMARY – CUSTOMERS

You must identify your customers' pain, and your passion for finding and curing it must link up with customers who are prepared to pay for having it cured. If you don't know what the customers' pain is, then you need to observe and interact with potential customers. Asking customers directly for advice is not always the best strategy. If you can ride with them, you can sell to them! If your answer is NO to any of the questions below, you need to keep on working with this gear.

QUESTIONS THAT REQUIRE AN ANSWER:

1 Have you found a pain that many potential customers share? (How do you know?)
2 Are you and your team passionate about curing that pain?
3 Do you know who your first customers are?
4 Can you make a prototype that resolves your customers' pain?
5 Will you be ready to cross the chasm when the time comes?

SYNC YOUR GEARS...SYNC WITH CUSTOMERS

Customers are where it all starts and ends! Everything you do from now must be synced with the wishes of your customers.

REMEMBER

Ride with your customers and understand their pain. Then develop a cure for it.

DELIGHT

WHY ARE YOU SPECIAL? THINK BEYOND
TO FIND YOUR DELIGHT.

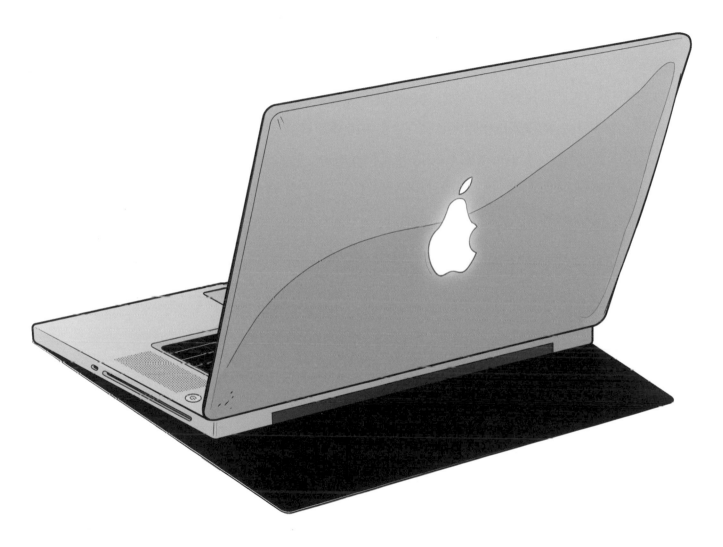

INNOVATE, DON'T IMITATE!

YOU HAVE FOUND YOUR FIRST CUSTOMERS AND SOLD THEM YOUR PRODUCT. BUT HAVE YOU "DELIGHTED" THEM? IN OTHER WORDS, HAS YOUR PRODUCT CHANGED THE GAME? IF SO, WHAT IS IT ABOUT YOUR PRODUCT THAT TAKES YOUR CUSTOMERS' BREATH AWAY? WHAT MAKES IT UNIQUE AND COMPELLING? ARE YOUR CUSTOMERS SO AMAZED BY IT THAT THEY WILL RECOMMEND IT TO EVERYONE THEY KNOW? WHAT MAKES THE EXPERIENCE OF BUYING FROM YOU SO INCREDIBLE THAT YOUR FIRST-TIME CUSTOMERS BECOME YOUR DIE-HARD FANS? PERHAPS YOU CALL IT YOUR COMPETITIVE ADVANTAGE. WE SAY IT'S THE DELIGHT.

PAY ATTENTION TO THE PYRAMID OF NEEDS

Delighting customers isn't easy. They don't want just a flashy presentation or a cool marketing stunt. They want you to cure their pain! So, to create delight, you have to start at the bottom of your customers' "pyramid of needs."

At an absolute minimum, you must provide functionality. This is the base of the pyramid of needs. Your product has to work if it's going to cure your customers' pain: A car has to get the driver from point A to point B. A remote control has to let the couch potato control the TV. A smartphone must let the customer talk, text, check e-mail, play games, etc.

The second level of the pyramid is efficiency. To make your product competitive, it must go beyond functionality and cure your customers' pain faster or cheaper (or both!) than anything else on the market. Does your car get great gas mileage? Can your remote control operate a TV, DVD, and home audio system without the customer having to use extra energy to get off the couch? Does your smartphone cost less than competing products?

Many companies achieve functionality and efficiency and then stop there. Look around! Me-too products clutter every market on earth. But functionality and efficiency alone are not enough to sustain success—and that is why many new ventures fail. Delight, at the pinnacle of the pyramid, is the

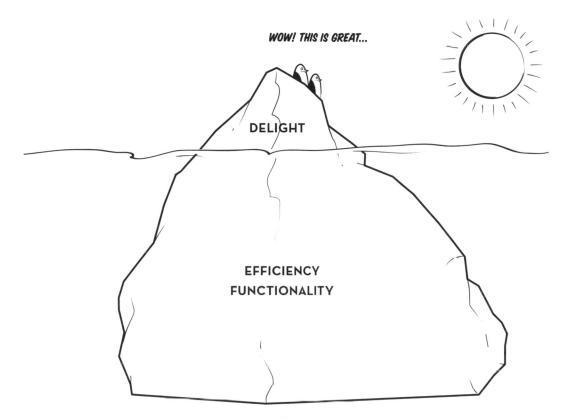

WOW! THIS IS GREAT...

DELIGHT

EFFICIENCY
FUNCTIONALITY

wow factor, the extra, unique attribute that raises your product head and shoulders above the rest. If you can create it, your customers will love you and never let you go.

INNOVATE, DON'T IMITATE

Delight is the result of relentless innovation. Delight must be invented or discovered. It is the "unique" in "unique selling proposition." It's the "compelling" in "compelling reason to buy." To create delight, you will constantly seek perfection, and you will never be quite satisfied. You will lie awake at night, searching your brain for the best way to cure your customers' pain. Without delight, your product is just a commodity—a foot soldier in the price wars, struggling to survive in a market where the big beats the small. With delight, your competition is in the rearview mirror. Delight can bring slow, sleepy markets back to life (think of how Apple's iPhone revolutionized the smartphone industry) or help you stand out in a crowd (like Zara, which is always first to market with the latest fashion at reasonable prices).

YOUR CUSTOMERS' PYRAMID OF NEEDS

TURN A NEED INTO A DELIGHT! WHAT IS THE WONDERFUL THING ABOUT YOUR OFFERING THAT DISTINGUISHES IT FROM OTHERS' OFFERINGS? THE HIERARCHY OF CUSTOMER NEEDS IS BASED ON FUNCTIONALITY, EFFICIENCY, AND DELIGHT.

My Delight:

Inspiration: "A car that can fly."

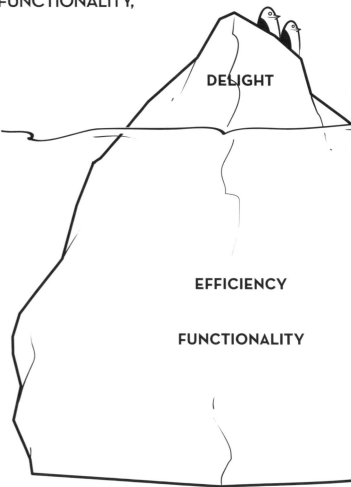

WOW! THIS IS GREAT.

DELIGHT

EFFICIENCY

FUNCTIONALITY

My Efficiency:

Inspiration: "Miles per gallon."

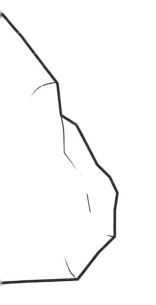

My Functionality:

Inspiration: "The car that will take me from A to B."

Note! *You need functionality and efficiency to be able to create delight.*
Inspiration: *Maslow's Hierarchy of Needs.*

BUT HOW DO I DELIGHT?

First, remember that if you can't ride with them, you can't sell to them. In the 1980s, Harley-Davidson faced stiff competition from Japanese motorcycle manufacturers. In a misguided attempt to simply keep up with the trend, the company decided to copy the Japanese manufacturers' approach and started producing high-quality, muffled motorcycles in all colors and sizes. The effort failed miserably, and the company had to undergo restructuring. What happened? The problem was that Harley-Davidson had not yet defined its delight. But when the board and the management team regrouped, they had an "aha" moment. They realized that Harley-Davidson was not in the business of selling motorcycles; it was in the business of selling a lifestyle.

A customer didn't have to be a Hells Angel to feel like one. As a Harley-Davidson executive famously said, "What we sell is the ability for a 43-year-old accountant to dress in black leather, ride through small towns, and have people be afraid of him." Once the company figured out that this was their delight, there was no looking back.

After you have correctly identified your customers' pain and feel that you thoroughly understand it, you can begin developing a cure. Look beyond everything that already exists in the market today and create something new that

you would love to use, a product that is "simple made easy." Capture the consumers' next, possibly unspoken, desire. If your product delights your customers, they will experience one pleasant surprise after another while they use it. They will feel like the product anticipates their needs. Sometimes they will find that it allows them to do things they could never do before. All of this makes using your product a pleasure. Customers will fall in love with it!

As you work on this, however, make sure that the delight you create is unique. It is certainly easier to simply copy what others are doing, but then why would a customer choose your product over anyone else's? Next, and equally important, make sure that your delight is difficult for others to replicate—because as soon as your competitors figure out how to copy what you are offering, your extraordinary delight dissolves into mundane functionality. Volvo learned this lesson the hard way. At a time when producing super-safe cars was not the highest priority for most auto manufacturers, Volvo chose to make safety its delight. Soon there was little question; if you wanted a reliable family car that would protect your children in an accident, you'd buy a Volvo. Today, however, safety is no longer a distinguishing factor because most vehicles produced by major auto manufacturers meet standard safety measures. As a result, what was once Volvo's delight—safety—became a functionality.

An exclusive, clearly identifiable delight will give you a sustainable competitive advantage. To achieve it—to break away from basic functionality and efficiency and create a delight divide—you need to be willing to take the lead. Answer the following to see if you are ready for the leap:

- What are you doing at the levels of functionality and efficiency to cure your customers' pain?
- Have you surpassed functionality and efficiency to delight the customer?
- Have you gone so far beyond the competition that you have changed the rules of the game?
- How do you keep it simple so your customers can tell stories about their delight to their friends and family?

If you find that you have not yet created delight, go back and work on your approach to curing your customers' pain. There's no point in moving forward until you get this right!

YOUR DELIGHT DIVIDE

HOW FAR HAVE YOU GONE BEYOND THE COMPETITION? HAVE YOU CHANGED THE RULES OF THE GAME? HAVE YOU INNOVATED BEYOND EFFICIENCY AND FUNCTIONALITY?

Explain why no one else can do it:

Inspiration: "Extraordinary product design and usability skills."

Note! Be honest! *Is your delight unique? Don't confuse it with functionality.*

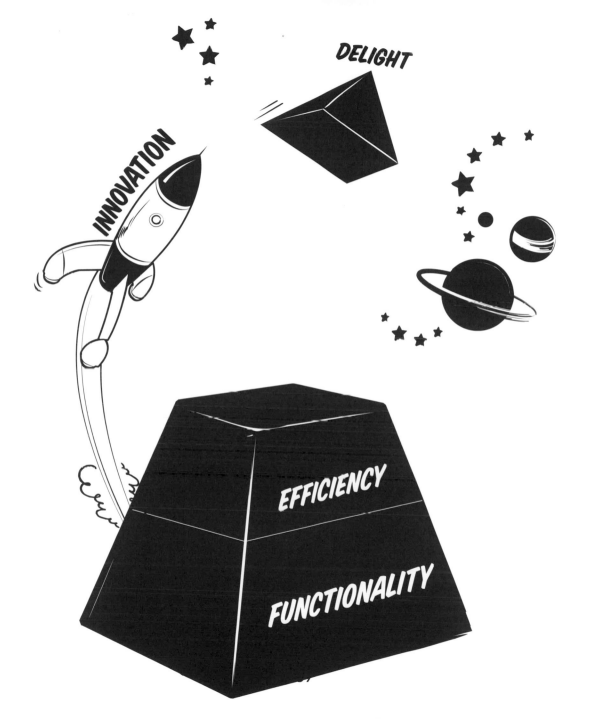

THE POWER OF STORYTELLING

Customers love to share their delight!

When customers buy a product, they discuss what they like and don't like about it with their friends. Those friends will listen closely and—unlike their response to even the best salespeople—they will trust what they hear. So what do your customers say about your product? What stories do they tell? How can you transform their most compelling stories into the stories that you tell in your own sales and marketing campaigns?

FRICTION-FREE STORYTELLING

You have 30 seconds to get a stranger to remember your product. Ready? Go! It's not a lot of time, is it? But it's all you've got to capture their attention and get them to say, "Tell me more." People love listening to stories that are authentic, entertaining, and new. A great story is never just informative; it also has emotional appeal. Always keep in mind that the story is not just about your product; it's about your customers' delight. The process of creating great stories is what we call friction-free storytelling.

THE STORY OF DELIGHT

Let's face it. Most stories are boring, forgettable, and not worth repeating. And because customers are people, and people are individuals, no single story will appeal to all of them. This is why you need to tell multiple great stories about delight. Never, ever tell a story that is not true! If your delight is successful, you will be well on your way to creating friction-free stories that will be retold millions of times.

Start by crafting two stories using different story lines. Here are proven story lines for inspiration:

- "My product is fighting a big, ugly enemy."
- "Richard Branson used it while skydiving!"
- "Larry Ellison loves it; Bill Gates hates it."
- "Brad Pitt and Halle Berry each bought one!"
- "It will help reduce global warming."

Next, try out the stories on your spouse or your mom or dad. After that, tell the stories to a couple of your friends and then to a pair of strangers. Finally, share them with the person in your life who can best play devil's advocate.

Did anyone buy both or at least one of your stories? If not, what caused the listener to resist being drawn into the stories? Where was the friction? Did people like one story better than the other? If so, what made one story more intriguing? Would they be willing to share either one of the stories with their friends? If not, ask them how they would change the stories to make them more compelling and then rewrite the stories based on their feedback. Your goal is to make the stories friction-free so that you can share them with prospective customers and your current customers will share them with their friends. Don't stop rewriting until you have a story that people love to tell.

DO YOU HAVE PROMOTERS?

Once you have polished and launched your friction-free stories, how can you measure how well they work? An easy way is to use the Net Promoter Score, a metric presented by Fred Reichheld and Rob Markey in their book *The Ultimate Question 2.0: How Net Promoter Companies Thrive in a Customer-Driven World.* The Net Promoter Score will help you find out how your customers feel about your product. Ask them to indicate on a scale of 0 to 10 how likely they are to recommend "X" to a friend or colleague. The ones who respond with a 6 or below don't like your product and will be your detractors. Those who rate it a 7 or 8 are indifferent to it. Those who answer with a 9 or 10, however, are thrilled with it and will become your promoters. Subtract your detractors from your promoters, and you will get your Net Promoter Score. If it is a positive number, you are successfully creating delight!

If you delight your customers, they will promote and sell your product for you.

Once you have created delight, your happy customers will turn into your volunteer marketing team and tell all their friends about your product. Because of their promotion, your product will essentially sell itself. In that case, your development team, rather than your sales force, will drive the bulk of the revenue growth. If you have failed to create delight, however, you had better be prepared to hire some hard-nosed salespeople. You'll need them.

Bottom Line
- If all you have is a functional, efficient product, then hire a massive sales team and work on customer acquisition.
- If you have achieved the delight factor, your development team will be thinking about sales in everything they do, and your customers will become your marketing team.

WOW! THE STORIES YOUR CUSTOMERS WILL SHARE!

YOU HAVE 30 SECONDS TO GET A STRANGER TO REMEMBER YOUR OFFERINGS.

The story you want your customers to share about your solution:

Inspiration: "Dropbox is the easiest way I know to share files with my coworkers."

How will the customers create buzz with your story?

Inspiration: "When they need to share a large file over the Internet, they will send an invite."

43

CREATING A FRICTION-FREE STORY

A GREAT STORY IS NEVER JUST INFORMATIVE. IT ALSO HAS EMOTIONAL APPEAL. REMEMBER THAT THE STORY IS NOT JUST ABOUT YOUR PRODUCT; IT'S ABOUT YOUR CUSTOMERS' DELIGHT. THE PROCESS OF CREATING GREAT STORIES IS WHAT WE CALL FRICTION-FREE STORYTELLING.

How can you create a friction-free story?

Inspiration: "The company and all their customers tell you the same story: Patagonia."

Note! Don't just tell stories! Ride with your customers and listen to their stories. It will help you develop a friction-free story.

THE CUSTOMERS' MIND-SET

WHY DO YOUR CUSTOMERS REALLY BUY IT? THINK ONE STEP BEYOND!

Are there unspoken things that are important?

Inspiration: "What we sell is the ability to ride through small towns and have people be afraid of you." – Harley-Davidson

outlaw
(Inspiration)

macho
(Inspiration)

show off!
(Inspiration)

belonging
(Inspiration)

Try to measure your delight:

Inspiration: "Net promotor score. Ask your customer to indicate on a scale from 0 to 10. How likely is it that you would recommend "X" to a friend or colleague?"

CHAPTER SUMMARY – DELIGHT

Without delight, your solution is just another forgettable product among thousands. With delight, complete strangers will love it at first sight. People spread the word about delight by storytelling. If you can discover or create a portfolio of friction-free stories, your customers, investors, channel partners, and even competitors will pass them along. Don't go any further with your business opportunity if you are not sure about your delight and your friction-free stories. If your answer is NO to any of the questions below, reframe the story for your customers until they are delighted and begin spreading the word.

QUESTIONS THAT REQUIRE AN ANSWER:

1 Do you understand your customers' pyramid of needs?
2 Have you created a delight that raises your product far beyond others?
3 Have you developed a family of friction-free stories?
4 Are your customers sharing the stories? That is, are you creating buzz?
5 Are you measuring delight?

SYNC YOUR GEARS...SYNC WITH DELIGHT

Be sure that your painkiller is a delight! The customer might not initially understand the painkiller. You might have to educate your customer and show them how to use it.

REMEMBER

Delight is all about innovation, not imitation.

CUSTOMER ACQUISITION

THE MOST IMPORTANT PART OF YOUR BUSINESS. HOW WILL YOU ADD MORE CUSTOMERS?

ALWAYS BE CLOSING!

EVERY MORNING, BEFORE YOUR FEET HIT THE FLOOR, THINK ABOUT HOW TO HOLD ON TO YOUR EXISTING CUSTOMERS AND HOW TO ATTRACT NEW ONES. EVERY DAY IS A BATTLE FOR CUSTOMERS. NEVER ASSUME THAT THE CUSTOMERS YOU HAD YESTERDAY WILL STILL BE THERE THIS MORNING. SINCE 100% OF YOUR REVENUE COMES FROM SALES, NO CUSTOMERS MEANS NO PROFIT AND, THEREFORE, NO FUN!

Focusing on customer acquisition is essential—it is the key to growing a business. To acquire customers successfully, you'll first need to understand what we call frequency and then balance frequency with two other equally important factors: delight and profit.

Customer acquisition is all about sales. Selling is hard, and the topic is not sophisticated enough to be taught at universities. Salespeople themselves see the job as either a curse or a calling. But every business has to have customers, and selling is the only way to acquire them. Sales is often underestimated; many companies assume that customers will just magically appear. We talk about frequency in sales because it is all about how many potential customers you contact, how many of those contacts will listen to your message and become paying customers, and how many of your customers will stay loyal.

No matter what you are selling—prepaid phone cards for a carrier? management consulting services?—you'll need to find a way of selling that both enhances your delight and keeps costs low.

There is a lot of mystique surrounding marketing and sales—understandably, since a company that's found a great way of acquiring customers won't want anyone else to copy it. But one thing is for certain; before you get to a yes, you will hear a lot of nos.

SALES: A NUMBERS GAME

Knock on 100 doors and perhaps 10 potential customers will open up to listen to what you have to say. Then, out of those 10 potential clients, maybe one will end up buying. But if you increase your frequency and knock on 200 doors, what happens? You'll probably close twice as many deals! Simply put, the more customers you contact, the higher the probability of a sale.

Some of you may now think, "OK, great, but I have an Internet venture, so selling is different for me! I don't need to hunt for customers. All I have to do is put my product online and customers will come to me." WRONG! Web-based products need frequency too! You may not be knocking on actual doors to offer your product, but you will still have to attract new visitors to your site via promotions on online forums and blogs, through catalogs and mobile advertising, and so on. The more time that potential customers spend on your site, the higher the conversion rate from random clickers to paying customers.

Great! Now let's see how you will do it!

THE PIPELINE MODEL

The process of acquiring customers can be described as a pipeline, and it starts with defining your leads: Who is most likely to buy your product? Whom should you approach? The more accurately you define your leads, the easier it will be to guide prospects through the pipeline and convert them into paying customers. But that's not all; meticulously defining your leads might increase the likelihood that those leads will become customers—thus resulting in a shorter pipeline—and lower customer acquisition costs. So put some serious thinking and research into defining your leads.

CUSTOMER ACQUISITION PROMISES

100% OF REVENUE COMES FROM SALES. NO CUSTOMERS MEANS NO PROFIT AND THEREFORE NO FUN. FOCUSING ON CUSTOMER ACQUISITION IS ESSENTIAL; IT'S THE KEY TO GROWING A BUSINESS.

Sales is a numbers game.
How many customers will you add next month?

Inspiration: "10."

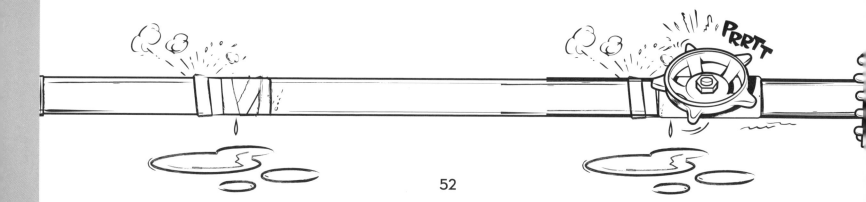

How many customers will you add over the next six months?

Inspiration: "100."

Note! Sales is all about frequency. How good is your frequency?

How many customers will you have in six months?

Inspiration: "I have 150 customers. I will add 100 and lose 50 = 200."

EXERCISE

DELIGHT IS PART OF THE PIPELINE

After you have identified your leads, you need to approach your potential customers, get that first meeting, and convince them that you have the solution to their pain. In other words, you must present the great delight you have developed—it's the best way to attract customers. But since your delight won't present itself, pay attention to your rhetoric and your sales pitch. Figure out how to explain your product in 30 seconds and under any circumstances (even in a crowded and noisy place). Then, work on your pitch again! If your product has a lot of functionalities, which one will you mention first?

Converting leads into paying customers is never flawless. There will be "leads" (potential customers who just don't want to talk to you any further) in your pipeline, and for some products the pipeline will be very long. Maybe you have to build trust with your potential customers, or maybe they don't have an immediate need for what you're offering. Maybe your internal sales cycles are too slow. Every pipeline is different!

PATCH THE LEAKS

Start watching the way prospective customers are funneled into your pipeline as early as possible. How many leads do you get per month? How many of them are lost immediately? How many are still there after the first encounter with the customer? How many contacts ultimately convert into paying customers? Once you understand how your funnel works, you can slowly start tweaking your system to patch the leaks.

And don't stop there! We can promise you that you are not done just because you understand your funnel. You will have to make mistakes, adjust things here and there, even start over again—all the while interacting with your customers and partners and creating a system that will be impossible for any of your competitors to copy (the secret sauce is safe!). Keep working and you will get there. How often you meet with your potential customers, where you do it, and the way you present your delight is all up to you.

ALWAYS DELIGHT THE USER

Pursuing frequency means looking for customers, interacting with them, and convincing them to buy your product. If you have created delight, however, you may not need to knock on customers' doors—they will be knocking on yours, begging to buy your product. This has three important consequences:

1   Delight reduces customer attrition.
Delighted customers are more loyal customers.

2   Delighted customers increase frequency and
reduce your sales costs. Customers who love your offering
will become your volunteer marketing and sales team and
promote your product through friction-free storytelling.
Because this effort costs you nothing and any resulting sales are on top of whatever your regular sales force
achieves, you can sit back and watch your profits rise.

3   Feedback from delighted customers will reveal a
lot about your product development efforts, and the more
conversations you have—i.e., the greater the frequency—the
more you will learn about how to enhance your delight. If
you listen closely and continue to perfect your product, it
will stand out from the competition even further. The lesson
here is clear: Always, always, strive to delight your customer!

SALES IS A TEAM EFFORT!
To achieve delight, the frequency team in your company has
to be in sync with the product development team, which in
turn has to be in sync with the customers. Orchestrating this
interaction is a critical task for your core team. How effective is your frequency team at helping your product developers create delight? To measure the team's effectiveness,
ask your customers to rate their interactions with people in
your company – you, the rest of the core team, your salespeople, and even your developers. Find out whether your
customers are happy with their experience and would tell
their friends and colleagues all about it.

ALWAYS BE CLOSING
Historically, selling has been seen as a battle for the customer's wallet, with the salesperson using every trick in the
book to close the deal—every salesperson's favorite moment. That's when salespeople think their work is done, and
it's up to the product team to deliver, the finance team to
invoice, and the customer support team to answer questions. Time to move on and capture new customers! But
sales are not really conflict situations. Rather, they're about
solving customers' problems and curing their pain. Since
the signature on the dotted line—hopefully—represents the
beginning of a long relationship with the customer, you
should never stop selling. The function of sales is not just to
acquire a customer. It's also to keep the customer.

LEADS

THE MORE ACCURATELY YOU DEFINE YOUR LEADS, THE EASIER IT WILL BE TO GUIDE PROSPECTS THROUGH THE PIPELINE AND CONVERT THEM INTO PAYING CUSTOMERS.

Where will you find your leads? What are the costs of securing leads, if any? List all the different ways to find leads.

Inspiration: "Referrals, communities, segmented lists, Google ads, etc."

How many leads will you lose immediately after the first contact?

Inspiration: "E-commerce web page; 80% of the visitors leave directly."

... FURTHER DOWN THE PIPELINE

AFTER YOU HAVE IDENTIFIED YOUR LEADS, YOU NEED TO APPROACH AND CONVINCE THEM THAT YOU HAVE THE SOLUTION TO THEIR PAIN. IN OTHER WORDS, YOU MUST PRESENT THE GREAT DELIGHT YOU HAVE DEVELOPED — IT'S THE BEST WAY TO ATTRACT CUSTOMERS.

What can you do to improve your sales pitch?

Inspiration: "What we sell is ..."

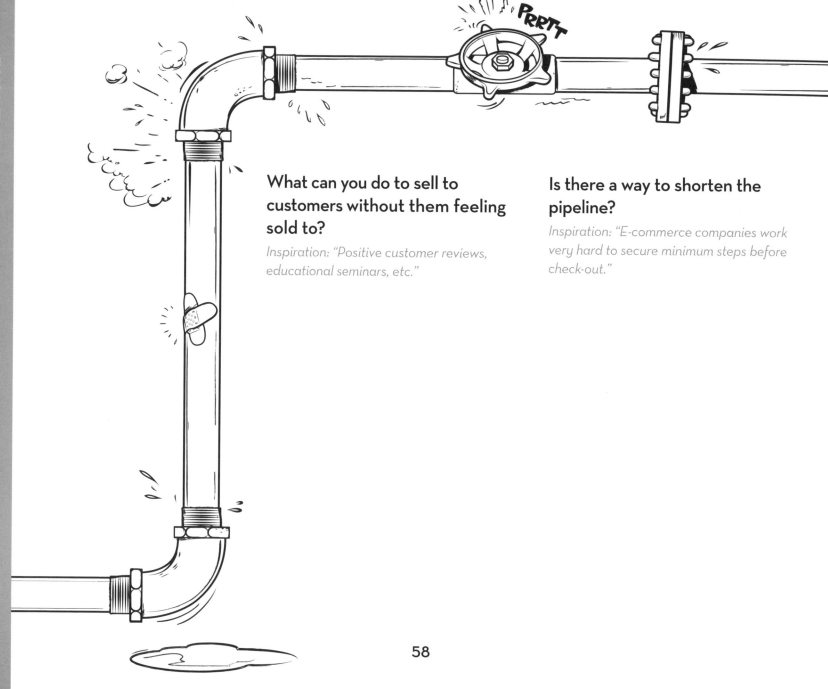

What can you do to sell to customers without them feeling sold to?

Inspiration: "Positive customer reviews, educational seminars, etc."

Is there a way to shorten the pipeline?

Inspiration: "E-commerce companies work very hard to secure minimum steps before check-out."

So far in the pipeline, have you convinced all the stakeholders?

Inspiration: "The customer and the user are not always the same."

Where do you have to patch the leaks so you don't lose customers during the sales process?

Inspiration: "The user appreciates the delight."

PROFIT

To accurately assess the role of profit in customer acquisition, you must consider three key questions. First, what is the cost of acquiring a new customer? Second, how many customers will leave after they try your product the first time? (That's known as the attrition, or churn, rate.) And third, what is the estimated lifetime value of your typical customer? In other words, how many items—whether they are add-ons, after-sales purchases, or additional months of service fees—will the average buyer purchase?

Costs

It's imperative that you know what the cost of selling will be as you grow. You'll need to assess how much each additional customer will contribute to the profit. Ask yourself: Do the benefits of gaining new customers outweigh my anticipated acquisition costs?

Figure out the total cost of customer acquisition (COCA), which includes sales, marketing, and ad campaigns. (Different businesses have different needs in terms of sales versus marketing expenditures. Make sure all your costs make sense.)

Rate of Attrition

Then determine your churn rate. Keeping your existing customers is as important as selling to new ones. If your churn rate is as high as your rate of new sales, there will be no growth in revenues. If you have a great customer acquisition team, you'll have many loyal customers and excellent growth.

Lifetime Value

Finally, figure out your customers' lifetime value (LTV), which is simply how much contribution you expect any given customer to generate over time. You should work to make sure that your LTV is higher than your COCA (and note that when it gets really high, you'll need to start scaling your business). If your LTV is much lower than your COCA, then you should tread carefully. And if it looks like there is no hope for your LTV ever to be higher than your COCA, then you have a problem.

Make sure to track your data methodically (initially you won't need fancy software for that; an Excel spreadsheet will do just fine). You'll want to include what was sold, who sold it, when, for how much, etc. You'll need this data when it's time to scale your business. Think about your idea and define how effectively you and your team are minimizing the cost of acquiring customers. What can you change to outstrip your competitors in decreasing acquisition costs and increasing customer lifetime value?

CREATE A UNIQUE SALES FORMULA

Great companies that have honed their sales tactics to perfection understand that executing sales efficiently means maximizing revenue and profit while delivering delight. Those companies ask, "What is our target market? How can we secure leads? How can the leads be converted into customers?" There are plenty of books, articles, and tools available that describe various ways to create a great sales culture within a company. But, ultimately, you will have to create your own unique sales formula for success. Note that the more unique your sales methodology is, the more difficult it will be for others to copy. That's important because your exclusive sales formula is your second line of defense—after delight—for maintaining market share. So even if your competitors manage to duplicate your delight over time, they will then have to continue working to decrypt your sales formula if they are to gain advantage over you.

Before you rush off to hatch your exciting new sales formula, however, make sure that you understand the one you've already got and replicate the things you have been doing

right. Recall where you found your existing customers and reflect on how you brought them in. Then make a list of the sources from which you got those customers. Determine which are the most rewarding; which brought in customers the fastest; and, most important, which are the most profitable. Do you see patterns that offer insights for future sales strategies? Are there potential challenges ahead? Once you've sorted out how you have acquired existing customers, rounding up more should be easy.

Now it's time to innovate—don't imitate! Look for newer, cheaper ways of delivering your delight. Strategize about how you can meet more customers, more often, and with more enticing offers. Use promotional channels in new ways to bring in more customers, reduce your customer acquisition costs, and make your sales even more unique. Every detail counts, from the very first contact through delivery, delight, and repurchase. How can you make tiny changes in process that quickly become overwhelming improvements in sales? In today's interconnected world, any event, no matter how seemingly remote or insignificant, may affect you substantially. A media mention, a simple meeting, even a post on Facebook could produce dramatic results. Think beyond your existing strategies and come up with new procedures where minor changes yield big returns.

Antonio Stradivari, a famous musical-instrument maker who lived from the mid-seventeenth to mid-eighteenth centuries, innovated to make the best violin in the world. The process he used to build his exceptional violins is so unique that it has not yet been replicated. When you create your sales formula, think of trying to build the best instrument you can, one that will both increase frequency and create delight.

EXAMPLE OF A GOOD SALES FORMULA

IKEA has taken frequency to an amazing level; the company constantly refines its sales formula. Consider the salespeople in an IKEA store. Do they seem like the typical, pushy sales team, herding you into their section of the store and trying to convince you that you need yet another lamp or a bed? Nope. Though the nice people in the yellow shirts are indeed part of IKEA's sales force, they don't actually "sell" to you. In fact, they have specifically been instructed not to. Rather, they just stand by, waiting for you to approach them for advice. Eventually—when you are ready—they will help you select the items you need. IKEA could have chosen to pack each aisle with sales bullies who wouldn't let customers pass without buying something, which might have maximized their short-term profit. Instead, they decided to work with frequency in a different way.

Anyone who has shopped in an IKEA store knows that it's never a fast trip. You know what you're looking for, but no matter what it is—napkins or light bulbs or whatever—you have to walk through all the other departments to get to it. (Yes, there are a few shortcuts, but still…) Every IKEA store in the world is designed this way. Why? Frequency! The enormous exposure to the store's goods increases the chance that shoppers will get the overwhelming urge to impulsively toss an unintended purchase (or 10) into their carts.

How many people go to IKEA with a shopping list and leave the store with everything they came to buy? Not many. Most shoppers can't find everything on their list and will need to go back again another day. Is that because IKEA has sloppy inventory practices? Of course not! It is part of their unique sales formula. Whenever shoppers have to return to the store, they are subject to the lure of impulsive purchases all over again and will probably end up buying more than they came for.

WHEN DELIGHT DECLINES, DO YOU INCREASE FREQUENCY?

Companies usually try to grow sales by increasing frequency. Often, however, the product eventually becomes harder to sell. What has happened? Over time, increasing frequency quietly expands a company's target market, and the old delight does not impress new customers. Setting up more meetings and trying harder to convince those customers to buy, therefore, just won't work. What you need to do now is listen to your salespeople, who are clamoring for adjustments to the product to meet new customer demands.

In other words, you need to start your product portfolio! This challenge often comes up when a company leaps from a single, small market to either several niche markets or one mass market.

So what do you do now? There is no need to abandon your first great product; it has its own delight, successful sales formula, and homogeneous set of customers, and you can continue to sell the heck out of it. But you do need to develop another great product, which will need a new delight, a different sales formula, and a modified profitability scheme to address the expanded customer base you have found. (Remember that whenever your target customers diversify or change, you will also have to change your frequency method.)

The product development team should not be the only group to undertake this challenge. Since the salespeople are the ones who talk directly to the customers, you'll want to make sure you maintain the feedback loop. Soon the accountants will come along as well and suggest that the sales and product development teams increase the price of the original product to cover the additional overhead.

Frequency must be balanced with delight and profitability for every single product your company offers. Without the skillful integration of all three components, your business may be headed for a fall. Imagine a three-legged stool missing a leg or two—the stool will topple over! There are no exceptions or excuses for failing to include all three elements. Just do it!

INNOVATING IN SALES

GREAT COMPANIES THAT HAVE HONED THEIR SALES TACTICS TO PERFECTION UNDERSTAND THAT EXECUTING SALES EFFICIENTLY MEANS MAXIMIZING REVENUE AND PROFIT WHILE DELIVERING DELIGHT.

What is your unique sales formula?

Inspiration: "IKEA has created a unique sales formula with exceptional store design."

Note! *Think about how effectively you and your team minimize the cost of acquiring customers. What can you change to outstrip your competitors in decreasing acquisition cost and increasing customer lifetime value?*

CHAPTER SUMMARY – CUSTOMER ACQUISITION

Customer acquisition is all about frequency, delight, and profit. Knock on as many doors as you can, and find a way to lower your sales costs. Take a close look at your pipeline. Make sure you delight your customers so they will remain loyal, promote your product, and deepen your delight divide. Consider the three components of profit: costs, attrition, and lifetime value. Have you created your unique formula for sales? If your product becomes harder to sell because your customer base has expanded, consider growing your product portfolio. Make sure each new product offers its own delight and has its own unique sales formula and profitability scheme.

QUESTIONS THAT REQUIRE AN ANSWER:

1   Do you understand your pipeline?
2   Is your sales formula unique?
3   Have you figured out how best to lower costs, reduce attrition, and maximize customers' lifetime values?
4   Do you have a team that understands the importance of balancing frequency with delight and profit for each product?

SYNC YOUR GEARS...SYNC WITH CUSTOMER ACQUISITION

Remember that your customers can sell for you! The best thing that can happen to you is if you can sign up your customers as part of your sales force.

REMEMBER

Close more deals by innovating in sales.

BUSINESS MODEL

GET PAID FOR YOUR EFFORTS

FROM IDEA TO CASH

EVERYONE NEEDS A BUSINESS MODEL. YOU WORKED HARD TO FIND AND DELIVER THE DELIGHT, AND NOW YOU NEED TO GET PAID FOR YOUR EFFORTS. BUT WHAT DO YOU CHARGE FOR, HOW MUCH DO YOU CHARGE, AND WHEN? INCREASE REVENUE AND LEARN TO PLAY THE ZERO GAME, REDUCING AS MANY COSTS TO ZERO AS POSSIBLE. EXPRESSING YOUR BUSINESS OPPORTUNITY IN NUMBERS WILL HELP YOU DETERMINE WHETHER OR NOT YOUR IDEA IS SUSTAINABLE. NUMBERS DON'T LIE. WITHOUT THEM, YOU WILL NOT BE ABLE TO TRUST YOUR PROGRESS!

Numbers are the most effective way of assessing a business opportunity. They provide credibility. If you understand your numbers, you understand your business. Are you hitting your targets? Have you identified the factors that affect them? Every tip suggested in the other gears of this book must be quantified right here in the business model gear. If you're not delivering on your plan, it's time to shift your approach.

Let's start with the zero game and then run through the basics. If you have an MBA in finance, you can skip the second part of this gear's description. By the same token, however, holding an MBA suggests that you probably haven't actually sold anything. In that case, we suggest you read about the customer acquisition gear again.

THE ZERO GAME

Costs are not inevitable. You can eliminate some of them! This might sound unbelievable, but dropping costs to zero—not just reducing them by 10% or whatever—is an important strategy. And the more innovative you can be, the better. Every zero that replaces a number in the costs column increases your chances of building a company that will one day change the world!

Challenge all the costs in your spreadsheet: Does each one deliver real customer value and delight? If not, then why keep it? Reduce it to zero! Take a particularly close look at the pieces that you consider to be non-negotiable simply because your competitors consider them non-negotiable. How can you turn existing costs into revenues? What would your customers say if you did? The zero game is about understanding your customers' pain, so make sure you have identified it accurately.

EXAMPLES OF PLAYING THE ZERO GAME

Several companies have successfully reduced some of their costs to zero. It will take innovation to reduce your costs that far, but every zero you create in the cost column increases the probability that the idea you're developing will be a game changer.

IKEA rises above the pack once again, this time as a skilled player of the zero game. The company changed the rules by challenging traditional methods of furniture sales. For example, they shifted the task of assembling furniture from the manufacturer to the customer. The result? IKEA was able to reduce assembly costs to zero in their spreadsheet while customers got the furniture they loved at a lower price. The move also cut store delivery costs, because individual furniture parts could be packed more efficiently than fully assembled items. And IKEA didn't stop there. The company then went on to realize savings on overhead costs by allowing customers to pick up their furniture directly from the warehouse. IKEA provided their

customers with delight through innovation in reduced pricing. Another company successfully playing the zero game is Skype, which supplies delight via free telephone services. The company's spreadsheet has a lot of zeros! If you play the zero game well, it will change the rules in your entire industry. Therefore, concentrate on challenging all the costs in your spreadsheet. Do your customers really need or want each item, or do you just assume they do? What can you reduce to zero while still creating delight?

Ryanair and Southwest Airlines also innovated in zeros, and they changed the game in the flight industry. For example, instead of paying fees to large airports for landing rights, they got smaller airports near major cities to pay them for their patronage. In addition, Ryanair converted the costs of handling luggage into a source of revenue by charging customers checked-baggage fees. Ryanair and Southwest were inspired by observing the services that bus companies provide to their customers. They realized that the only significant difference between the two modes of transportation is that airlines offer a much faster ride. Lesson learned: If you want to challenge existing structures and business models, look at companies outside your own industry. Innovation is as important in the business model as it is in creating and expanding delight.

HERE ARE YOUR ZEROS

COSTS ARE NOT INEVITABLE. YOU CAN ELIMINATE SOME OF THEM! DROPPING COSTS TO ZERO, NOT JUST REDUCING THEM BY 10%, IS IMPORTANT.

Describe your zeros:

Inspiration: "IKEA changed the rules by challenging traditional rules of selling furniture. They were able to reduce assembly costs to zero and now customers get the furniture at a lower price."

Where?

Inspiration: "IKEA shifted the task of assembling furniture from the manufacturer to the consumer."

Whose resources?

Inspiration: "IKEA cut delivery costs by 80% since individual furniture parts could be packed more efficiently than fully assembled items."

Why?

Inspiration: "IKEA provided their customers with delight through innovation in reduced pricing."

Note! *If you are in an existing company; how can you reduce your cost by 90% without losing your delight?*
To achieve a goal like this you must start doing things you have never done before.

WHAT IS THE CUSTOMER PREPARED TO PAY?

Calculate your price using one of two methods.

1 Cost-based pricing: With this technique, you figure out how much it costs to develop, manufacture, and sell your product. Then you add a margin to cover other costs in your company and to increase your profit, and set your price accordingly. You want your margin to be in line with those used by companies similar to yours—very much a traditional and well-accepted method of pricing. Cost-based pricing makes comparison very easy for both customers and competitors. Customers may especially challenge you on the margins in a business-to-business setting. And while you can try to be discreet about your margins, customers will eventually figure them out.

2 Value-based pricing: Here your price is determined simply by how much you think your product is worth to customers. Your assessment has nothing to do with the costs of developing, manufacturing, or selling the product.

If you are curing your customers' pain, are successfully creating delight, and have differentiated yourself from your competitors, then you should always aim for value-based pricing. If you end up with cost-based pricing, you will be locked in to your price by whatever margin you set. Keep in mind how many times you've heard people say, "I would have paid more for it!" A low price is not always the right strategy.

Many companies don't even dare try to use value-based pricing, however. If you offer a standard product with no clear delight, then you might want to base your price on cost to remain competitive. But if your delight factor is high, you can easily base your price on value instead.

WHAT IS YOUR PROFIT? HOW BIG ARE YOUR LOSSES?

Now that you have set the price, you can start working on your profit and loss (P&L) sheet. Start with revenue—the fun part! To find out if and when you might see an increase in revenue, multiply your price by the number of customers you expect over the next three years. This task is easily done with a simple Excel spreadsheet, but it is where most companies fail in their calculations.

Next is cost: You need an office, phone service, insurance—all examples of overhead costs. Add in salaries and cost of equipment for development, manufacturing, etc., and then calculate revenue minus costs for the next three years. Don't be discouraged if you foresee only losses at first; many high-potential companies stay in the red for several years. Consider securing external funds to bridge those first years.

CUSTOMER ACQUISITION DATA

Take a close look at the data you've been tracking for your COCA and LTV.

Check to see that you have entered data on the product sold, the name of the salesperson, the date of purchase, market price, etc. Remember that you will need this data to assess whether you are allocating resources properly and that it will be invaluable later on as you start to scale. Make sure your pricing is in line with your sales structure. For example, you can't expect to have an outside sales force pursuing customers if the average deal is less than $10,000. The math won't work out in the long term if your COCA is always higher than your LTV.

Start watching the shape of your customer pipeline as early as possible. How many leads do you get in a month? How many turn into real opportunities? How many of those opportunities convert into paying customers? How many of

those customers will remain loyal to you and buy more than once? When you understand your pipeline, you can slowly start tweaking your system to fix the leaks and ensure that you'll get more sales.

WHAT NEEDS TO BE DONE TO BE SUCCESSFUL?

You've done the numbers, and that's good! But are your numbers realistic? Experience (your own or someone else's) and metadata (e.g., how many people in a certain geographical area, income level, gender) will help refine your estimates. The more effort you put into the numbers, the closer to reality you should be able to get.

After the calculations are done, it's time for a more difficult job, which is to implement a plan that will make the numbers come true. You need to run what's called a sensitivity analysis. Start by asking yourself, "Based on the figures in front of me, which factors will have the greatest impact on the venture's future success?" Sales numbers and customer acquisition often stand out as the key attributes to focus on, but there is so much more that demands proper attention. How do you distinguish between what you must have and what you might just like to have?

PRICING STRATEGY

HOW MUCH DO YOU THINK YOUR PRODUCT IS WORTH TO YOUR CUSTOMER?

Is your pricing strategy cost based ...

Inspiration: "Manufacturers of concrete add a margin to cover the cost and set the price accordingly."

Explain why:

Inspiration: "Products from manufacturers of concrete are very similar. There is no clear delight. The products are standard and homogeneous."

... or value based?

Inspiration: "Apple bases their prices on how much the products are worth to the customer."

Explain why:

Inspiration: "Apple has created a delight and has differentiated themselves from the competition."

SHOW US THE NUMBERS!

BY NOW YOU SHOULD HAVE A SPREADSHEET. WHERE ARE YOUR NUMBERS?

Gordon Gekko was here

	year 1	2	3
Number of customers			
Price/sold unit			
Total Revenues			
Variable cost/unit			
Customer Acquisition Cost			
Fixed Costs			
Total Cost			
Total Revenue – Total Cost= Earnings before interest and tax (EBIT)			

When you wonder about adding more costs, pursuing a fresh opportunity, or entering a new market, don't forget to ask a fundamental question: "Will spending time and resources on this item make a significant difference for the company?" When you're in doubt about spending money to get new customers with a marketing campaign, or buying new chairs for the development team so they don't call in sick because of their aching backs, go back to your calculations. Problem solved!

SET GOALS

To be able to gauge whether you are spending your time and resources wisely, ask yourself, "What do I plan to accomplish and by when?" Some might call this defining your strategy, but we just say that you need to state your goals! The purpose of setting goals is to foster a shared understanding and cohesive behavior within the company. However, simply setting and sharing goals is not enough. You also need to practice what you preach by defining the path to reach those goals.

There are three common pitfalls when setting goals. First is trying to define goals that are too numerous, too vague, or so complex that no one understands them. The second pitfall is underestimating the importance of visualizing and communi-

cating the goals to the rest of your team.

The third pitfall is setting goals based on unclear information. If ambiguity negatively influences the data collection process, you could end up unsure about whether you need to adjust your time and resources at all.

Make the goals simple to grasp and the measurements easy to translate into daily activities. Clear and concise definitions of the goals are critical for boosting performance. You don't want key figures stumbling around in the dark when they're trying to, say, facilitate the collection process.

Now go ahead and define a few quantitative goals. Remember that what gets measured gets done! Remember also, however, that not everything can be a goal. Some objectives may be important and worth measuring but are not goals themselves. Think of owning a car. Your goal for buying it might be to drive fast, but you'll need to make sure that there is air in the tires, oil in the engine, and gas in the tank if you're going to get anywhere. Regular car maintenance helps you achieve your goal, so you don't want to neglect it, but there's no need to take any additional action until something changes—like the need to put on snow tires in the winter.

After you have defined and communicated your goals, keep your executive committee meetings focused on them. Collateral departments, such as finance, should only be heard from if a situation arises that calls for action.

Remember to continuously monitor whether the company is progressing in line with the goals.

SET GOALS

THE PURPOSE OF DEFINING GOALS IS TO FOSTER A SHARED UNDERSTANDING AND COHESIVE BEHAVIOR WITHIN THE COMPANY. HOWEVER, SIMPLY STATING AND SHARING GOALS IS NOT ENOUGH.

What are your goals and how should they be communicated?

Inspiration: "Reach 1,000,000 customers. Kick-off and big signs."

What are the most important things that should be measured?

Inspiration: "A sports car dashboard consists of torque and speed."

How can they be translated into daily activities?

Inspiration: "We must add 2,740 customers a day to achieve that goal within a year. With a 1% conversion, that means 274,000 new leads to be contacted every day."

Note! *Some objectives may be important and worthy of measuring but are not goals themselves. Think of owning a car. Your goal for buying it might be to drive fast! But you'll need to make sure that there is air in the tires, oil in the engine, and gas in the tank if you're going to get anywhere. Regular car maintenance helps you achieve your goal, so you don't want to neglect it, but there's no need to take any additional action until something changes—like the need to put on snow tires in the winter.*

MOVE YOUR NEEDLES

TO BE ABLE TO GAUGE IF YOU ARE SPENDING YOUR TIME AND RESOURCES WISELY, ASK YOURSELF "WHAT DO I PLAN TO ACCOMPLISH AND WHEN?"

What will really move the needle to success?

Inspiration: "Increase the number of customers."

What will really move the needle into the red (losses)?

Inspiration: "We lose a distribution partner, or costs for sold items double."

What should you do then?

You'd better figure it out ...

HERE ARE YOUR REVENUE STREAMS

CAN YOU EARN MORE MONEY ON WHAT YOU ARE OFFERING, I.E., HOW CAN YOU FIND YET ANOTHER REVENUE STREAM THAT COULD ALSO INCREASE YOUR DELIGHT?

How?

Inspiration: "Ryanair increased revenue by selling snacks on the airplanes, charging for luggage, and creating partner deals with parking lots, rental cars, and transportation to remote airports."

When?

Inspiration: "Today? Tomorrow? Next quarter?"

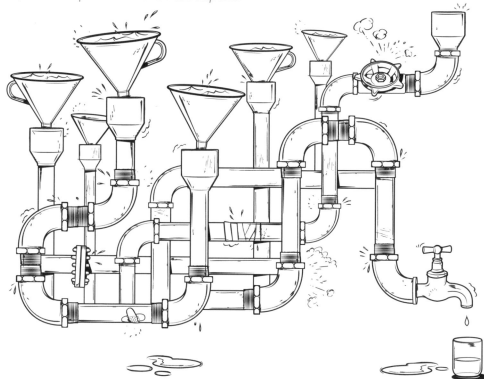

CHAPTER SUMMARY – BUSINESS MODEL

Crunching the numbers helps you strategize your pricing, determine future investments, and estimate the growth path of your company. Strive for zeros in the cost column of your spreadsheet. Create a killer customer acquisition strategy and aim for value-based pricing with a unique delight. Define a few clear goals and communicate them to your team. Monitor your team's time and resources constantly so that everyone is on track to achieve those goals.

QUESTIONS THAT REQUIRE AN ANSWER:

1   How well can you play the zero game?

2   Have you decided on the right pricing strategy?

3   Do you have all the data you need to calculate your costs?

4   Have you set a few clear goals for your business?

5   Are you monitoring your time and resources and making adjustments as necessary?

SYNC YOUR GEARS...SYNC WITH BUSINESS MODEL

Your business model is so much more than just about the numbers! Always strive for your business model being part of your delight.

REMEMBER

Cash is generated by great ideas and innovation in creating zeros.

PARTNERS

NO COMPANY IS AN ISLAND.

WHO LOVES YOU, WHO HATES YOU?

THE CHALLENGE IS NOT JUST TO FIND PARTNERS, BUT TO FIND THE RIGHT PARTNERS. TO DO THAT, YOU MUST FIRST ASK YOURSELF, "WHO LOVES ME? WHO HATES ME?" SECOND, YOU MUST CONSIDER YOUR POTENTIAL PARTNER IN TERMS OF REVENUE AND DELIGHT AND DETERMINE THE VALUE THAT THOSE PARTNERS MIGHT OFFER YOU. THIRD, YOU AND YOUR PARTNERS MUST DECIDE WHAT EACH OF YOU WILL GIVE TO THE PARTNERSHIP AND WHAT YOU WILL GET OUT OF IT.

A successful partnership will spur growth in revenues, profits, market share, and the value of your brands. But there's a catch (of course). Sometimes doubling the delight divide, which accelerates your profits, will put your partner's business model into a tailspin! It's absolutely essential to understand how joining forces with you will affect your potential partner's bottom line before you call to ask for a meeting.

NO COMPANY IS AN ISLAND

Partnerships are crucial for the growth of your company, and you can create them for many aspects of your business—manufacturing, R&D, product development, sales, distribution, and customer support. You need partners! In our rapidly changing world, product cycles shorten as companies focus, specialize, and differentiate their core missions while outsourcing tasks to partners. No company, large or small, has cured all their customers' pains without partners. **Don't ever try to do it all by yourself!**

WHO LOVES YOU? WHO HATES YOU?

Finding the right partners, however, isn't easy. In the beginning, you may be so flattered by the first company to show interest in your business that you jump to form a partnership. Or maybe you dream about joining forces with one of the big brands in your industry: "How can we fail if we partner with Walmart or Mercedes-Benz?" Unfortunately, even the most eager or most famous business may not be the best partner for you. To create a lasting partnership, both partners must be able to achieve their objectives more effectively by working together than by working separately. Fame and affinity have little to do with partnership success.

Partners fall into two categories: Those who love you and those who hate you. Why would you ever partner with someone who hates you, you may ask? Because you may not be able to tell which is which at first! Your shiny new partner may start out looking like a perfect fit and then morph into your arch-enemy later. It happens!

Love: Partners who truly love you will want you to succeed. Why? Because your success increases their success! First of all, working with you will increase their revenues and profit. Second, working with you will help them identify or deepen the delight divide that captivates their customers. You might be giving them new weapons to use against their competitors, decreasing their customer acquisition and retention costs, reducing their time to market, or improving the quality of their products and services. Finally—and most important—if your partners' customers love you, your partners will love you even more! So find out what hidden pain your potential partners' customers might have and then help find a cure for it. When potential partners hear their customers' stories of how you helped solve their problems, they will be eager to sign on the dotted line!

Hate: Partners who grow to hate you often have compelling reasons for doing so. After all, even a tiny new player can inflict great pain on its partners. Consider that terrific new offering you just developed, for example. Your partners' customers were languishing with an awful, unidentified pain—until you came along and cured it. When you entered the market, therefore, you not only showed your partners what they should have done a long time ago, but you also changed the rules of the game! Suddenly their customers are demanding things like lower prices, better service, added features, faster shipment, and so on—all of which costs money and creates hassles that your partners would have preferred to avoid.

YOUR ENEMY'S ENEMY IS YOUR FRIEND

Potential partners really hate it when you threaten their existing revenue stream, and they loathe the delight divide that you have uncovered. Worse, they may think that they can't even beat you by joining you because it will annoy their current partners and blow a hole in their business model. They may even be working with one of your competitors!

The most difficult situation for a potential partner is when they love you, but their customers hate you. Skype's experience provides a good example of this. When Skype was first introduced, handheld-device providers were happy to partner with Skype. Skype's claim that the "whole world can talk for free" didn't bother them because their customers'

customers had to buy handsets to make all those calls. The problem was that the device manufacturers' customers—wireless carriers—hated Skype. All that free calling cannibalized their profitable long-distance business.

Whether a company loves you or hates you, therefore, sometimes has nothing to do with you. It's all about the intricate relationships among other players in their ecosystem. Key points? When considering potential partners, think about how partnering with you will affect all their other partnerships. And keep in mind that once you've successfully brought one partner to the table, others will follow more willingly.

WHAT CAN YOU GIVE AND WHAT WILL YOU GET?

In any relationship, but especially in business, you have to give something to get something in return. In a partnership, each side is betting that pooling their resources will increase their revenues and profits faster than if they worked alone. And each partner usually ventures stakes that it holds in abundance, hoping to get back stakes that are rare and difficult to imitate. The better the partners complement each other, the more valuable the partnership is for both sides. The contract for the deal, however, is not enough to create a sustainable partnership. To deliver the promised delight to customers, partners must continually work to keep alive a mutual understanding of their gives and gets. If that understanding dissipates and one side decides to go with a new, different solution, the partnership will wither and die. Consistency and dependability are essential for creating a successful partnership.

EVERY PARTNERSHIP STARTS WITH A YES!

A young company's first partnership can be very exciting. It's wonderful to know that someone out there is interested in what you're up to! But before you start celebrating your new collaboration, you should evaluate it along two dimensions: revenue and delight. Your partner should either help grow your revenue (whether directly or indirectly) or increase the possibility of offering a unique and sustainable delight to your customers—or both! Most partnerships will produce at least some benefits along each dimension, but those benefits may not be in equal proportions. You should always feel optimistic about your partnerships. The strongest partners will help you secure revenue and develop your delight equally well.

PARTNERS

PARTNERS ARE CRUCIAL FOR THE GROWTH OF YOUR COMPANY. FINDING THE RIGHT PARTNER, HOWEVER, ISN'T ALWAYS EASY.

List the companies that ...

... love you:
Partners who truly want you to succeed.

... hate you:
Partners who grow to hate you often have compelling reasons for doing so.

Note! *Your enemy's enemy is your friend.*

REVENUE-DELIGHT MATRIX

EVALUATE EACH TYPE OF PARTNERSHIP CAREFULLY TO ENSURE THAT YOU MAKE THE BEST ALLIANCES.

PLACE POTENTIAL PARTNERS ON HOW:

1. They contribute to your revenue (with numbers if you can!) and/or delight (describe!)
2. You contribute to their revenue (with numbers if you can!) and/ or delight (describe!)

It's OK...

... if you don't know the names of potential partners.

... to straddle between different types of partners.

... if you don't know where to put a partner. Put them in Yes!

... to put the same partner in different squares.

PARTNER'S POTENTIAL TO SECURE REVENUE

Jurassic Partners · Love or Hate · Strategic

Spam Partners · YES! · Ammo in a War

Poison · Playmates · Learning Partners

PARTNER'S POTENTIAL TO HELP YOU DEVELOP YOUR DELIGHT

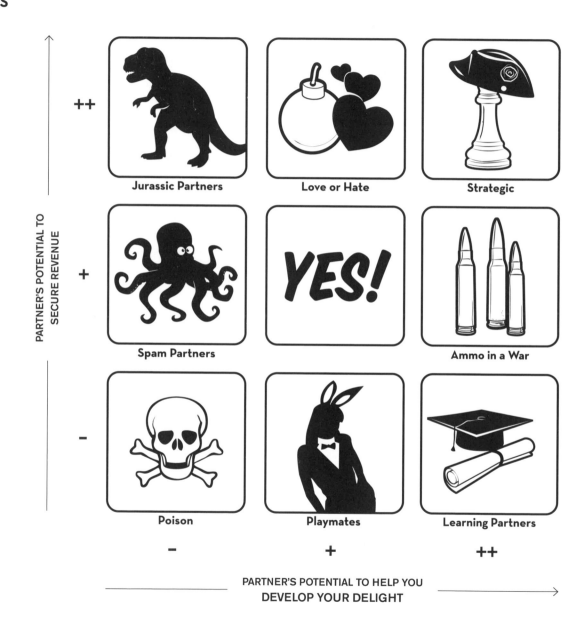

PARTNER'S POTENTIAL TO SECURE REVENUE

++
Jurassic Partners · Love or Hate · Strategic

+
Spam Partners · YES! · Ammo in a War

-
Poison · Playmates · Learning Partners

- · + · ++

PARTNER'S POTENTIAL TO HELP YOU
DEVELOP YOUR DELIGHT

MAKE SURE THE SHOE FITS

There are many different types of partnerships. Evaluate each type carefully to ensure that you make the best alliances.

PLAYMATE PARTNERS

Playmate partners offer little in the way of revenue but do help spread the word about the delight you offer. Over time, however, you are likely to outgrow this kind of partnership. Think of it this way: If you and your first partners don't play in the same league anymore, then they are no longer adding to your business, and you are not getting any return for the energy you spend on them. It's time to look for new partners! But that doesn't mean you have to sever all ties with your old buddies. Feel free to take their calls and keep their logos on your website—just don't waste any more resources on them.

LEARNING PARTNERS

Learning partners help you better understand your product, your market, and your value chain—all necessary for growth and success—and they add great value along the delight dimension. They are important allies who can also contribute to your company's friction-free storytelling. Typical learning partners are universities, organizations that innovate in products, and seasoned entrepreneurs. There is no risk in

adding a learning partner—you can learn something from anyone. The challenge lies in quantifying just how much you have learned from these partnerships. And since they usually don't offer anything significant in terms of revenue, you can probably do better.

SPAM PARTNERS

Spam partners add money to your coffers by disseminating your product to a large market with minimal costs. But they can be a nuisance because they add frequency indiscriminately, and potential customers will either ignore them or, worse, become irritated by them. This is not a very sophisticated way to acquire customers. Keep looking!

AMMO IN A WAR

Sometimes you are the ammunition in someone else's war! What does that mean? It means your product helps another

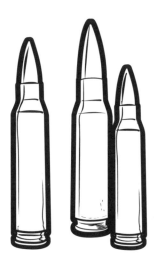

company fight off its competitors. So how is this kind of partnership useful to you? Well, for starters, this partnership delivers value along both the revenue and delight dimensions. Your product will reach a larger target audience, and thus bring in revenue, when your partner distributes your merchandise as an add-on to their goods. You also gain access to that company's large customer base with little cost when its customers realize that they also need your product. Essentially, you are parachuted right into the heart of a new market and your product is repositioned to provide another unique delight. These partnerships are perhaps the hardest ones to identify and assess—and serving as ammunition in someone else's war can be intimidating—but the experience can be quite rewarding. Work closely with this partner.

JURASSIC PARTNERS

Jurassic partners—think of Walmart and IKEA—are the juggernauts of your market or industry, and these merciless players can change the rules of the game in a heartbeat. So imagine having them in your partner portfolio! If your product has a delight that they need to bundle with their product, your revenue could go through the roof. And as long as you have them on your side, you will be the envy of all of your competitors. But be careful! If Jurassic partners really love your product, they can go from being your best partner to your worst enemy by developing their own similar product and integrating it into their solution. They can also destroy you easily when they no longer enjoy your company. If you fail to deliver or someone else starts providing the same service for less money, you'll be toast! Jurassic partners will always do what is in their best interest—not yours. Make sure that your delight is communicated whenever they are involved and that you are really their partner, not just their vendor.

LOVE OR HATE PARTNERS

Because you don't always know whether your new partner will come to love you or hate you, foreseeing the future of a love or hate partnership can be difficult. The big question is, do you trust this partner? Love or hate partnerships don't

stay consistent over time; partners who grow to love you may become strategic partners (a good thing!). But those who end up hating you may turn into Jurassic juggernauts. To help figure out which way the partnership is headed, try to determine whether you are an equal contributor to the collaboration or a pawn in your partner's other games. Monitor these relationships carefully and protect your position as they change.

STRATEGIC PARTNERS

In a successful strategic partnership, both sides will enjoy significant benefits. The gives and gets are clear, and the partners are similar in size and influence. But what happens if, say, you are a new company and 80% of your revenue comes from your big, influential partner, but your product only amounts to 1% of your partner's revenue? In that case, you will need your partner more than your partner needs you, and you are not likely to rate the attention or resources you'd need to help the partnership become strategic. You may even end up in a Jurassic partnership. Strategic partners are generally a very elite group.

POISON PARTNERS

These partners are the exception that prove the rule. Avoid them at all costs! Of course, you would never initiate a partnership with someone who looks like a bad bet from the start, but you should assume that some great potential partners will prove to be poisonous. When you realize that the partnership you were about to form has huge drawbacks, offering little (if any) benefits in revenue or delight, gracefully withdraw from the negotiations. Make sure you exit on a friendly note, however. Even poison partners may prove beneficial to your cause further down the road, and you may need to approach the same candidate again at some point.

Use the Partner Give-Get Matrix when getting ready for negotiations with either an existing partner or a new one. We have filled out the matrix (in gray) using the example of a mobile operator partnering with a gaming company. When you use the matrix, replace the information in the cells with the details that apply to your particular situation.

FROM YES TO STRATEGIC

IN A SUCCESSFUL STRATEGIC PARTNERSHIP, BOTH SIDES WILL ENJOY SIGNIFICANT BENEFITS.

Explain how your partners could become strategic partners:

Inspiration: There is a clear give-get. The partners are similar in size and influence.

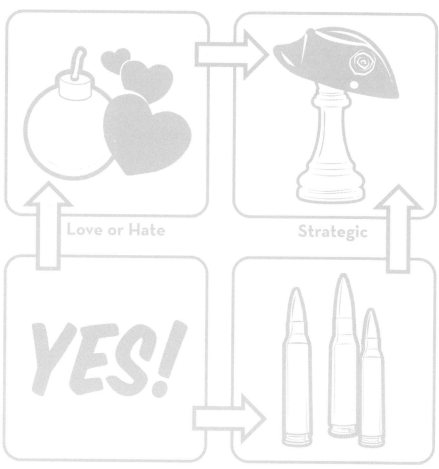

Love or Hate

Strategic

YES!

Ammo in a War

YOUR PATH TO YOUR PARTNER

YOU KNOW WHOM YOU WOULD LIKE TO PARTNER WITH. YOU NOW NEED TO FIGURE OUT HOW TO REACH THEM!

The name of the partner: _____

Whom do you know?

List all the people you know with connections to the partner.

What will you tell the gate-keeper (i.e., the person who can give you access)?

What will convince the gate-keeper to let you talk to the decision-maker?

What will you say to the decision-maker?

Who will make the decision? You have 30 seconds to get their attention!

How will you say it?

E-mail, phone, face-to-face?

THE PARTNER GIVE-GET MATRIX

POTENTIAL STAKES TO BET ON THE PARTNERSHIP	PARTNER CAN GIVE Mobile Operator ☞ Gaming Company	PARTNER CAN GET Gaming Company ☞ Mobile Operator
Technology (product, platform, and process technologies)	Access to infrastructure	New content
Resources (money, time, talent, and knowledge)	Money	New products
Relationships (with customers, channels, investors, government)	Distribution channel	Content providers
Reputation (visibility, credibility, brand equity)	Stable, big	Fun image
Delight (learning, adding value to the product)	The world's biggest operators offer the games to their customers	Always the latest and coolest games for the operator's subscribers
Factors that can make or break a partnership	Access to customers	More revenue from customers
Chemistry of key people (culture, character, personalities, values)	Understanding local culture	Understanding younger demographic
Company vision and strategy (purpose, mission, values)	Growth	Youth market

CHAPTER SUMMARY – PARTNERS

Partner or perish! There are three things to consider when identifying partners. First, ask yourself who loves you and who hates you. Second, how will each potential partner contribute to your revenue and delight? Third, what will you and your partner give to and get out of the partnership?

QUESTIONS THAT REQUIRE AN ANSWER:

1 Do you know who loves you and who hates you? Do you know why?

2 Are you ready to embrace the partners who love you and protect yourself against those who hate you?

3 Do you know how your partners will contribute to your revenues and delight?

4 Do the gives and gets produce a clear and compelling value proposition for both you and your potential partners?

SYNC YOUR GEARS...SYNC WITH PARTNERS

Make sure that your partners succeed when you do! The perfect partner will always contribute to increasing your delight divide and introduce more customers to you.

REMEMBER

All partnerships are about love or hate.

COMPETITORS

DON'T BE INTIMIDATED BY THEIR EXISTENCE. BUT BE AWARE.

BIG BEATS THE SMALL OR FAST BEATS THE SLOW

COMPETITION NEVER DIES. MAYBE NO ONE IS TRYING TO SELL A PRODUCT EXACTLY LIKE YOURS IN YOUR MARKET, BUT YOU DO HAVE COMPETITORS: ALL BUSINESSES COMPETE FOR CUSTOMERS' TIME AND MONEY. THE QUESTION YOU NEED TO ANSWER IS, "WHAT ELSE COULD MY POTENTIAL CUSTOMERS SPEND THEIR TIME AND MONEY ON?"

What, you don't agree? You think you don't have any competitors? There are three possible responses to your position:

1 You are mistaken! (This is most likely the case.)
2 You have identified an opportunity that is so small no one else wants to pursue it.
3 You have identified a great opportunity in a hidden market, and your idea is perfect for it. You are a genius!

Or… not. If a scenario sounds brilliant, then you can bet that others are thinking about it. And even if you are alone now, you won't be for long. For most companies, competition is all too easy to see.

One of our colleagues claims that "There is no competition until you make more than $10 million in revenue." What he really means is that unless you are a large corporation, you don't need to pay too much attention to your competitors. You will want to be aware of them and keep an eye on what they're doing, of course, but don't waste any time or resources on them—and certainly don't try to copy them.

What you should be focusing on instead is adding delight to your product. In fact, if you create a truly incredible delight, you'll blow away your competitors!

DOES THE BIG BEAT THE SMALL? OR DOES THE FAST BEAT THE SLOW?

One way to figure out how much to worry about your competitors is to determine the type of market you are in. Ask yourself, "Does the big beat the small, or does the fast beat the slow?" In other words, are you fighting for your life in the storm-tossed, shark-infested seas of a Red Ocean, or are you swimming peacefully in the calm waters of a Blue Ocean? The terms "Red Ocean" and "Blue Ocean" were coined by W. Chan Kim and Renée Mauborgne in their book *Blue Ocean Strategy*.

RED OCEAN

In a Red Ocean, you are one among many companies offering pretty much the same product, and you are all just trying to survive. Your challenge is to convince potential customers to switch away from a product they've been buying from someone else, perhaps for years, to your product.

The good news for fish in the Red Ocean is that the rules and alliances are already established. If you are new on the scene, you can easily size up the situation and learn the ropes. The tricky part is that you can't stay a newcomer for long: You have to grow up fast, because in a Red Ocean, the big beats the small. A company in a Red Ocean market has to work on exploiting existing demand. Ask yourself, "Which customers can I poach from someone else? How can I convince them to buy this product from me instead of the company they're used to buying from?" You will need to add delight by making your product a little bit cheaper, faster, or better so customers will make the shift. Then align your company with the value proposition you've chosen, and outperform your competitor!

BLUE OCEAN

In a Blue Ocean, the water is clear and clean because you are pretty much the only fish swimming in it. It is not stained with the blood of competitive battles because no one has discovered your market (yet!). Imagine—no competition! Sounds wonderful, doesn't it? Unfortunately, it's better in theory than in practice. Why? Because a new product in a new market has no demand, so you will have to create demand. Think about that. You want people to buy a product that they have never heard of and don't understand, and you are asking them both to re-evaluate what might be a long-standing purchasing decision and then change their behavior. That's a tall order—and you'll have to educate your customers to achieve it—but you can do it. After all, inventing a set of terms to explain the new product you're offering is not so difficult.

To completely succeed in the Blue Ocean, however, you will need to pursue differentiation and low cost. Think back to the pyramid of customer needs. In terms of functionality and efficiency (the bottom two-thirds of the pyramid), a Blue Ocean company's product might be the same as a Red Ocean company's product. The difference between the two lies in the delight factor (the top of the pyramid). Success in the Blue Ocean will depend on offering a delight that is completely different from comparable offerings in the Red Ocean. Remember that the greater your delight, the harder it will be for other companies to copy it—and that's a sustainable advantage for you.

DETERMINE THE TYPE OF COMPETITION

IN THE MARKET SPACE THAT YOU ARE TRYING TO CAPTURE, IS IT THE FAST THAT BEATS THE SLOW OR THE BIG THAT BEATS THE SMALL? FUNDAMENTALLY THERE ARE TWO TYPES OF MARKETS THAT WILL DETERMINE THE TYPE OF COMPETITION YOU ARE FACING. ARE YOU SWIMMING IN A RED OR A BLUE OCEAN?

RED OCEAN

Check the box that best applies to your business and explain why.

☐ You are competing

☐ You are beating the competition

☐ You are exploiting an existing demand

☐ You have made the value/cost trade-off

☐ You have differentiation or low cost

▷ ☐ You are a complement

▷ ☐ The competition is irrelevant to you

▷ ☐ You are creating a new demand

▷ ☐ You have broken the value/cost trade-off

▷ ☐ You are solving a problem in a new way

BLUE OCEAN

ARE YOU AN OUTPERFORMER? OR ARE YOU A GAME CHANGER?

If you are comfortable in Red Oceans, you will spend your days trying to wrestle away customers from established incumbents. To succeed in a Red Ocean, therefore, you will have to be an outperformer and just be better than everyone else in your market. It's an uphill battle, and your success will depend on your ability to power up with long-lasting batteries and stay focused until all your competitors have either surrendered or died. Always remember that this is a test of focus and endurance; if you look away for just one second, or your batteries are not fully charged at the start, your competitors will win.

Things are different in a Blue Ocean; there you are a game changer. You might be the only player in sight, a market may or may not be established, and the rules are still undefined. You can afford to look away for a second without losing anything because you have no competitors yet. In this case, your mission is to create a product that goes so far beyond whatever is currently available. If you can do that, then sit back, relax, and watch the customers stream to your door. You won't have to lift a finger to attract them—they'll be standing in line to get their hands on your product! Game changers, as one entrepreneur explained, "get customers even when

the office is closed." That, of course, is the good news. The bad news is that your batteries better be the longest-lasting ever made, because Blue Oceans always turn into Red Oceans, and you will have some big fish to fight!

Consider the cell phone market. It used to be that if you wanted to talk on the phone, you had to use an instrument that was plugged into the wall—and that's where you were stuck until your conversation was finished. But then cell phones arrived; all of a sudden, you could walk around, get a snack, and even travel while you chatted away. The delight factor was huge! But even though people loved this new convenience, cell phones were seen, purely and simply, as a complement to the Plain Old Telephone System—which was where the outperformers ruled. Because getting rid of landlines in favor of cell phones hadn't occurred to anyone yet, big established carriers and phone manufacturers essentially ignored the new market.

Eventually, however, the cell phone phenomenon grew large enough to attract the attention of the established outperformers, and the game changers in the cell phone market started to feel fierce competition. At about that time, a little fish broke away from the battle and swam in a different direction. Powerful incumbents laughed at the small fish for lame ideas like adding a larger screen and eliminating the traditional keyboard. But the little fish staked out its territory and kept on working to improve the delight factor, eventually establishing a whole ecosystem on its own and becoming famous. The name of that once-small fish? Apple!

Most companies strive to be outperformers, and many of them rely on a differentiating factor to increase their likelihood of survival. Some of those companies would like to wake up one morning as game changers. If that sounds like you, take a minute to look very closely at who you really are. Do you have what it takes to become a true game changer? Or are you at heart an outperformer just dreaming of changing the game?

THE INNOVATOR'S DILEMMA

An outperformer will eventually be "beaten" by a game changer; it is just a matter of time! Clayton Christensen is one of the authors who has best described the challenges of being what we call an outperformer, and what happens when game changers disrupt or create markets. His research has shown that outperformers will always be outcompeted by game changers; it is only a matter of time.

Why does it happen? Plain and simple: The game changer's

disruptive technology or innovation upsets the existing order of things in a particular market. Usually, it starts with the game changer appealing to the low-end customers of the market, i.e., those who previously haven't been able to afford or access what has been offered in the market.

This is all well and fine for the outperformers in the beginning. They may tell themselves and each other that the game-changing activities introduced by that small start-up in a barrack at Stanford will never take off. They might go so far as to say that the likelihood of the game changer succeeding is the same as "when pigs fly." But rest assured, the game changer will start hurting the established companies! It starts hurting when the customers of the existing solutions realize that there is a simpler product (without bells and whistles) in reach.

The challenge for the outperformers is that they don't generally react to what the game changer is doing until it is too late. Why don't they react? Because no one else in the market is reacting, neither their competitors nor their partners are paying attention because it is out of their scope. The outperformer is focused on serving the demand of its existing customers, on moving its product further by using incremental innovation. But over time, customers start to challenge the bells and whistles offered to them and are keen to switch to the simpler and cheaper solution, putting the outperformers out of business.

Imagine going up in the mountains for a day of skiing: Traditionally that meant putting your skis on and slowly—and maybe painfully—ascending the mountain one breath at a time. At the top, a few well-carved turns and you're at the bottom again. Few people enjoyed that experience completely, but more became interested on the day when the possibility of using a train to ascend the mountain was introduced. Of course it was a little bit troublesome—take off the skis, wait for the next train, etc.—but it worked. Then the first lift was introduced; cheaper, more convenient. But you still have to wait in line and maybe take several lifts to reach the summit for that nice off-piste adventure. Imagine if there was a lift that could fly you up to the top within a few seconds! And imagine it's free, and ready to take off whenever you're ready to go up again?

The interesting thing is that the mountaineers who invented the first equipment to access and climb mountains did not invent the mountain train. The train companies did not survive the chairlift companies, and it will probably not be a chairlift company that invents a flying air chair. That innovation will likely come from a different place, if it will ever arrive.

 P.S. Remember, most game changers fail, but one day there will be one that succeeds …

GAME CHANGER OR OUTPERFORMER?

YOU WILL CHANGE THE GAME AND MAKE COMPETITION IRRELEVANT. YOU WILL CREATE A NEW DEMAND AND SOLVE EXISTING PROBLEMS IN A BETTER AND CHEAPER WAY. OR YOU WILL OUTPERFORM THE MARKET AND BEAT COMPETITION IN AN EXISTING GAME. NOW YOU HAVE TO PICK SIDES. YOU CAN'T BE BOTH AT THE SAME TIME.

You are a game changer. Explain why:

Inspiration: "Apple's iPad was a game changer."

You are an outperformer. Explain why:

Inspiration: "Samsung exploits existing demand by copying functionality and adding better efficiency."

WHO CAN BEAT YOU?

WHAT COULD YOUR OFFERING BE COMPARED TO? THINK ABOUT THE DELIGHT YOU OFFER! WHO ELSE COULD YOUR CUSTOMERS TURN TO, TO GET (ALMOST) THE SAME THING?

The customer could turn to ...

Inspiration: "A Mercedes-Benz could be switched for an Audi."

Was it hard to find competitors?

Because ...

Inspiration: "The Audi is solving the same pain as the Mercedes-Benz."

COMPETITION NEVER DIES

MAYBE NO ONE IS TRYING TO SELL A PRODUCT EXACTLY LIKE YOURS IN YOUR MARKET, BUT YOU DO HAVE COMPETITORS: ALL BUSINESSES COMPETE FOR CUSTOMERS' TIME AND MONEY.

With the money spent on your product the customer could ...

Inspiration: "For the cost of one high-end branded bag the customer could get 20 low-end bags in different colours."

With the time spent on your product the customer could ...

Inspiration: "Instead of going to the movies for two hours the customer could play a video game or visit a café."

Note! Think you don't have any competitors? There are three possible responses to your position: 1. You are mistaken. (This is most likely the case.) 2. You have identified an opportunity that is so small no one else wants to pursue it. 3. You have identified a great opportunity in a hidden market, and your idea is perfect for it – hats off! You are a genius!

OUTPERFORMER		GAME CHANGER
TRADITIONAL ACADEMIC LITERATURE	⇄	**GEAR UP**
Delight the author	⇄	Delight the readers
Star performers	⇄	A circle of authors
The thicker the better, strive for 500 pages, with a lot of words and many examples	⇄	About 200 pages with a lot of illustrations; short and consistent
Academic/Top management audience	⇄	Everyone with a business/idea is the audience
Academically rigorous	⇄	Best of ivory tower and street smart
The truth	⇄	A complement … to different truths
Provide depth	⇄	Provide inspiration
Unrelated books, in size and concept	⇄	Same concept and format
Paperback	⇄	Educational platform
The author is a time teller	⇄	The authors are teachers of clockbuilders

RED OCEAN STRATEGY	**BLUE OCEAN STRATEGY**

CHAPTER SUMMARY – COMPETITORS

You will always have to compete for your customers' time, money, and attention, whether now or in the future. If you swim in a Red Ocean, bulk up and decide on your strategy—either greater value or lower cost—and then get ready to outperform your rivals. If you float in a calm Blue Ocean, quickly focus on your delight while offering differentiation and lower cost. Become a game changer so customers will come to you. Then, when your Blue Ocean turns red, either secure your position so you become big and unbeatable or swim away to a new Blue Ocean.

QUESTIONS THAT REQUIRE AN ANSWER:

1 If you swim in a Red Ocean, are your batteries charged?

2 Do you know how you will outperform your competitors?

3 If you swim in a Blue Ocean, have you created a phenomenal delight?

4 Can your offering turn you into a game changer?

SYNC YOUR GEARS...SYNC WITH COMPETITORS

Competitors are people too! Many are the competitors that could be turned into excellent partners.

REMEMBER

A small game changer can beat a big outperformer, but a powerful, established incumbent can crush a quick newcomer. It all depends on whether the ocean is blue or red.

GO GLOBAL

SCALING YOUR BUSINESS BEYOND BORDERS.

GOOD IDEAS HAVE
NO BOUNDARIES

GOOD IDEAS KNOW NO BOUNDARIES. ANSWER THE QUESTION POSTED IN THE PREVIOUS CHAPTER BEFORE YOU CAPTURE THE WORLD: ARE YOU A GAME CHANGER OR AN OUTPERFORMER? BECAUSE—TRUST US—IT MAKES A HUGE DIFFERENCE WHEN YOU ARE GOING GLOBAL.

SCALE YOUR BUSINESS

You'll need to consider many factors as you decide whether or not to expand your company. For example, can you use your current sales formula in new locations? If your customer delight is universal, then you're already ahead of the game. But if it is designed to meet your local customers' needs, then you'll have to adapt your product to the new markets. Will the composition of your team need to change? Most likely, it will. You will need to incorporate complementary skills, which means hiring people who are fluent in different languages, familiar with other cultures, and perhaps come from diverse backgrounds. This transition can be a challenge for current team members. Individuals who previously had strong positions on the team might have to move to more supporting roles, and everybody will need to adjust to a new infrastructure, revised processes, maybe even a larger building that is better equipped for your expanding venture. If so, don't be surprised when you hear grumbling about the "good old days"; it's common for workers in this situation to completely forget about how they used to be crammed in small offices with little heat, no air-conditioning, and cheap furniture. It's all right to let them grumble—at least for a little while. They will adjust eventually.

If you are serious about going global, you should keep three important points in mind. First is that the process will take much more time than you probably think! In fact, we suggest that you double the amount of time you have planned for.

Second, be careful not to underestimate the amount of energy that going global will consume. You will have to balance everyone's excitement about exploring new ideas and markets with the need to keep things running smoothly in the office back home. This is not easy! Our suggestion: Plan on quadrupling your current level of energy.

Third, make sure you constantly monitor the progress of your expansion and be both ready and able to end it if necessary. Yes, we know you are certain that the market you want to exploit actually exists; you've got a Gartner report showing it, your consultants have confirmed it, and your gut feelings are almost always right. But sometimes things just don't fall into place the way they should. And while scaling back on your original plan could feel like failing—and you might have to endure an I-told-you-so or two—stubbornly going forward against the odds would be a huge mistake. Go home, lick your wounds, learn from your mistakes, and try again.

...GO GLOBAL FOR A GAME CHANGER AND AN OUTPERFORMER - HUGE DIFFERENCE!

As you should already be aware of—if we have done an OK job!—it is a tremendous difference to be a game changer or an outperformer. Even though there is a lure to suggest that you are both, we strongly oppose such a view and encourage you to go "all in". That helps both your work with your business opportunity and your path, speed, and ambition to go global.

A game changer is in the business to make a change, to disrupt, to revolutionize. When you go global, it is therefore not a lot to try and learn from how existing business

have conquered countries and captured markets. Instead you have to create from the beginning. Imagine that you have a white piece of paper and you have to start drawing what will be your go-to-market plan in different parts of the world—many of which you have no pre-knowledge of which might be a good thing! There is an opportunity to be able to decide who will be involved in your business abroad (go back to the Partner chapter), how you will go about it, and how you will design the whole endeavor. The creation of how you will change the game in an established market or how to create a new one is an important part of being a game changer.

When an outperformer goes global the way to do it is different: Then it is of importance to pay close attention to how comparative businesses have done it before and to—just—do it a little bit better than those who are already there.

For both game changers and outperformers, it is of value to have an understanding of the: who, what, and how?

SHOULD YOU STAY OR SHOULD YOU GO?

PUT A STAR IN THE COLUMN THAT BEST MATCHES THE CRITERION. CALCULATE HOW MANY STARS YOU HAVE IN THE THREE DIFFERENT COLUMNS. THE TOTAL GIVES YOU A CLUE TO THE ANSWER TO THE QUESTION.

CRITERIA	GO GLOBAL!	DON'T KNOW	STAY LOCAL!
Customers and Pain (Most target customers are based outside our country and the pain is global)	☆		
Delight (Our delight is global)		☆	
Business Model (Advantages can be leveraged in other markets)		☆	
Partner (We have partners who love us)			☆
Competition (It is important to move fast before anyone else does)	☆		
Go Global (Our leaders have unique global skills and networks)		☆	
Team (The team's vision is to build a global company)			☆

GOOD IDEAS KNOW NO BOUNDARIES

YOUR ABILITY TO EXPLORE GLOBAL OPPORTUNITIES IS VIRTUALLY LIMITLESS.

Imagine what your venture might look like if you expanded around the world.

Inspiration: "Apple, Google, Samsung, Vodafone, Coca-Cola, Porsche, and many more have done it."

121

NEXT STOP(S)

YOU HAVE DECIDED TO GO GLOBAL. LET'S LOOK AT A MAP AND DECIDE YOUR NEXT STOP! IF YOU'RE NOT CONVINCED THAT YOU SHOULD GO GLOBAL, THAT'S FINE. MAYBE THE EFFORT IS NOT WORTH THE RISK OR YOU DON'T WANT TO SCALE. IF YOU ARE UNCERTAIN: GO BACK AND REVIEW THE GEARS AS IF THE WHOLE WORLD WAS YOUR MARKET.

1 **Mark the place on the map to show where you are going to go next**

   Inspiration: "Sao Paulo."

2 **How big is the market you want to target?**

   Inspiration: "From Sao Paulo I want to target South America."

3 **Ask someone from somewhere else!**

   Inspiration: "Who should you ask to help you   open the South American market?"

GOING GLOBAL MEANS UNDERSTANDING PLAYERS, STAKES AND CODE

In order to go global and capture global markets, you need to understand how things are done "over there". It's hard enough to understand markets that you are very familiar with, but imagine trying to do so in a country where people speak another language and hold very different expectations for your product, your company, and your team.

You will do so by becoming familiar with the Circles of Influence, i.e.,—players, stakes, and provincial code—in those new markets you are exploring. Players are the companies, institutions, and people important for your success in a new country. Stakes are the things you must bring to the new market in order to be taken seriously—and money alone is not enough. Finally, you need to comprehend the provincial code, or how business is done in the new place. When you fully recognize all three components, you are in the sweet spot, ready to go places!

PLAYERS ARE THE VIPS

It's easy to assume that institutions, organizations, and other important players abroad will have the same standing as similar entities at home. But trust us, this is rarely the case! The role played by an entity at home might be played by a different type of entity abroad—or maybe not played by anyone at all. Keep an open mind when pursuing tasks in your new environment—even if it looks (pardon the expression) completely foreign to you.

Important players everywhere can be categorized as either local or global players. A local player is well known and has a good reputation within its region but is relatively unknown outside of it. Lightspeed Venture Partners, in Silicon Valley, is a good example of a local player. Global players, as one might expect, are well known around the world; PricewaterhouseCoopers is an excellent example of a global player. The trick is to know when, why, and how to use which one. It would be a mistake to assume, for example, that global players are always better than local players, or vice-versa. What's more, different ecosystems operating within the same location may rate players differently. So pay attention! Make a list of the top-notch players you think will be important for your venture and then work on how to get to know them.

PLAYERS BET THEIR STAKES

You will need table stakes to play the game in a new place. Money, of course, will be important, but as we have cautioned, it is often not enough. So what kind of nonmonetary stakes can you offer? First is delight, which will open doors for you! While those multinationals we mentioned were getting nowhere, for example, small start-ups offering terrific delights were getting Cisco's and Intel's attention. Second is talent. If you can show that you are ready to use and share a particular, extraordinary knowledge that you possess (for instance in technology, marketing, or business execution), then you are also demonstrating that you are willing to put something at stake. Third is customer relations. If you are prepared to risk your reputation with your existing customers, then you are also putting something at stake. And if your stakes can be turned into an advantage for someone else, then you will pop up on the radar of the important entities in your new location—and those new connections can then be leveraged into relationships with the big players. Now, to the list of players that you have created, add the stakes that you will risk.

LEARN THE PROVINCIAL CODE TO GAIN ACCEPTANCE

The rules for "correct" behavior vary from place to place, and the provincial code prescribes the etiquette for conducting business in a certain environment. The roots of the provincial code are found in the overall culture, traditions, and values at play. If you understand and follow the provincial code, you will earn people's trust, integrate more quickly into the environment, and have less anxiety about encountering challenges and difficulties. The easiest way to learn the provincial code is to shut up, look around, pay attention, and ask local friends and colleagues what you can ask for, how to ask for it, and so on.

Knowing your opponent is the most important thing in a battle! Contact the local chambers of commerce and other country- or industry-related organizations for information. Don't forget your college roommates, backpacking travelers, and your Facebook friends, too. They probably all have stories to tell that will help you learn the ropes. But why should they help you—what's in it for them? Maybe an invitation to your product launch in the new location!

YOUR CUSTOMIZED LONELY PLANET

We can't advise you on whom to contact, what to bet, or how to behave in certain places. Our assumptions and preconceptions will not help you keep an open mind as you develop your strategy for going global. But filling out the following table might help you determine your next steps.

THE WHO, WHAT AND HOW

What place are you going to?

_____

Inspiration: "Sao Paulo."

	PLAYERS Players are companies, institutions, and people of importance for your success in a new country.	**STAKES** Stakes are what you bring to the new market in order to be taken seriously.	**CODE** You need to comprehend the provincial code, or how business is done in the new place.
What I know	_First class incubator where I can get a desk and a phone._	_Money can always take me a little bit further._	_Never number my business plans when giving them to VC._
What I need to know	_Who can help me with viral marketing?_	_How can I use my reputation from doing business in Europe?_	_How do I know whom to trust?_
How I can get to know	_Call my roommate in college._	_Set up my first meeting with Heinz and listen to what they expect._	_Go to a Chamber of Commerce meeting._

Note! _Forget about the money you need, the travel arrangements you have to make, and the shots you need to take._

CHAPTER SUMMARY – GO GLOBAL

Going global is the big prize! But it comes with big risks; you'll need more money and more people, and you might have to call off the game unexpectedly. Have faith that you can do it, but at the same time be humble. The players, stakes, and provincial code in different parts of the world will influence your business and how successful you will be.

QUESTIONS THAT REQUIRE AN ANSWER:

1 Is there a global market for your pain?
2 Have you determined whether going global would be a good idea for your company?
3 Do you know where your next market will be?
4 Do you know how to identify the circles of influence in the new place?

SYNC YOUR GEARS...SYNC WITH GO GLOBAL

Oh, the beauty of being able to offer a painkiller that is for the whole world! Always strive to sync your gears so you can go global.

REMEMBER

Good ideas have no boundaries.

TEAM

YOU CAN'T DO THE "WHAT" WITHOUT THE "WHO."

GET THE RIGHT PEOPLE ON THE BUS

"SO, WHAT DO YOU DO?" IS THE FIRST QUESTION THAT MANY PEOPLE ASK ABOUT A NEW VENTURE. BUT "WHO'S ON YOUR TEAM?" IS AN EQUALLY IMPORTANT QUESTION. YOU CAN'T DO THE WHAT WITHOUT THE WHO, AND YOU CAN'T DETERMINE THE WHO WITHOUT THE WHAT! FROM DAY ONE, MAKE SURE THAT ASSEMBLING YOUR TEAM IS A TOP PRIORITY.

It's all about "getting the right people on the bus," as Jim Collins observed in *Good to Great*. Think of your company as a bus, and imagine that you're going on a road trip. You have a rough idea of where you're heading, though the route may change along the way, but who will you bring with you? Your team must encompass world-class, dedicated talent; have the ability to deliver; think in a non-linear, out-of-the-box kind of way; and include five key personas.

THINK WORLD-CLASS TALENT!

Without the right talent, your company can do nothing. The education, training, experience, and aptitude of each person on your team will add to your company's core assets. Surround yourself with world-class, dedicated talent, and you can start up your bus.

ABILITY TO DELIVER

All the talent in the world will get you nowhere without the ability to deliver. Highly talented people with terrific skills are useless if they can't work with their teammates or if they crumble under pressure! This road trip is not for quitters—everyone on board will have to adapt to changing road maps, tight deadlines, setbacks, and launches. To get your bus moving, make sure that the world-class talent you found can deliver the goods!

NON-LINEAR CREATIVE THINKING

The masterminds of a business opportunity excel in combining the vision for their company with a large dose of passion. With this non-linear thinking, they help their company create its destiny. Non-linear thinkers challenge existing truths and time-tested solutions. They work outside the box to determine when and how the not-yet-invented will be discovered. Non-linear thinking will prevent your bus from driving around in circles!

FIVE KEY PERSONAS

To maximize the three core attributes above, make sure that

they are encompassed in five key personas: the innovator, the evangelist, the producer, the administrator, and the integrator. All are critical. If you're missing even one persona, your team will be incomplete.

THE INNOVATOR

First in line is the person whose flash of genius will spark the whole enterprise. Think Sir Isaac Newton, Thomas Edison, Bill Gates, and Steve Jobs, all of whom mastered the art of non-linear thinking in their fields. If your team has an innovator as extraordinary as anyone in that group, then you are good to go. But if you're like the rest of us, don't worry—there is still hope! Some of the best innovations bring new life to ordinary, everyday problems or offer a fresh take on a tried-and-true solution.

THE EVANGELIST

It takes a very particular kind of individual to grab a concept, leap out of the plane with eyes wide open, and talk about it all the way down while taking care to land in the right place, at the right time, and with the right equipment. This uniquely deranged, yet essential, persona is the entrepreneurial evangelist. Passion, vision, and a nothing-is-impossible attitude allow the evangelist, even after a crash landing or two, to transform the innovator's idea into a fully-formed venture.

Just as religious evangelists must sell the idea that becoming a follower will lead to divine peace and happiness, the entrepreneurial evangelist has to convince the team, customers, investors, and other stakeholders that this new venture is the true route to the pinnacle of business success. So what makes a good evangelist? An evangelist must care passionately about customers' pain (often at the expense of time with friends and family) and be creative about how to cure it. Flying economy class, staying in cheap hotels, and eating nothing but instant noodles—this is the way evangelists live. In their view, money is for moving projects forward. It is not wasted on silly things like comfort.

For evangelists, seemingly impossible tasks are perfectly logical, and the road ahead is clear. Evangelists are the spin doctors of growth; they can tell a really good story about any product, and the story is usually so amazing that the people who listen are delighted to retell it to their friends. An evangelist can fall, get up, and keep moving forward without missing a beat. Evangelists realize that mistakes are part of the game because each misstep brings the team closer to the solution. Not that evangelists love mistakes (who does?), but good evangelists are prepared to face them, learn from them, and even accept the blame for them.

Running a compay is stressful—a failing one even more so. Will the product ever work? Do we have enough money to make payroll? Will someone steal our intellectual property? Evangelists live in a world full of those questions yet remain graceful under fire. They show optimism and a sense of humor when all seems lost, convincing employees and investors to stay the course and weather the storm.

THE PRODUCER

Innovators and evangelists are great at starting businesses. But sustaining a successful launch requires someone who knows how to turn an idea into a tangible product or service. This magical being is the producer. It is one thing to

put an idea on the drawing board, turn it into a prototype, and show it to a small set of first customers. It is quite another to develop processes for churning out mass quantities of the product over and over again, and for revising those processes when the product is updated. The producer appreciates the repetitive nature of delivery in large quantities and understands the importance of logistics and operations. Perhaps above all, the producer takes pride in developing an efficient chain of production, anticipating possible interruption, and preparing for future changes.

THE ADMINISTRATOR

If innovators, evangelists, and producers understand one another's complementary talents, they'll work well together in the "garage phase" of the company and take the new venture a long way toward the ultimate goal. They may even be quite happy with themselves and with their accomplishments—until they get their first real order and the company begins to shift from a garage-centric approach to a growth-centric approach. Once the celebrations are over, start growing!

Growth problems arise when you need more people on the team to continue doing business. Adding more staff means defining new roles, outlining more tasks, revising old methods, and filling out mountains of paperwork.

This is a difficult time for everyone, but especially for innovators. Their lovely, idyllic vision now has to align with real-world goals. If that tarnishes the patina of perfection, so be it; the company must grow or perish.

It's time to bring in the administrator, who will provide structure for a world where chaos has reigned. The administrator will demand schedules, budgets, and follow-up plans—much to the horror of the original dreamers. But along with the binders, databases, and administrative resources comes a much-appreciated sense of serenity as well.

That peacefulness might even last a while. But eventually, even while the producer is busily connecting the dots and implementing the tasks, the innovator and evangelist will again see the light (most likely a different light!), and frustration will start to rise anew. A good administrator will soon realize that individual parts of the organization are following different paths and that functions have been fully optimized. Before everyone stumbles under the pressure, bring in the final persona – the integrator.

THE INTEGRATOR

At this point, the company needs a center of command, someone to negotiate among different departments, respond to changes, and focus on overall strategy to keep the whole organization on the same page. For example, suppose the goal is to build a coliseum. The innovator has come up with a tremendous vision, the evangelist is spreading the word with fervor, and the producer has started to figure out that they're going to need construction materials and suppliers. The administrator is happily working on the rules, pulling building permits and establishing fair working conditions for the employees.

Overseeing all these efforts is the integrator, who carefully pays attention to every aspect and coordinates the various functions quickly and efficiently. When the innovator wanders off—"Ditch the coliseum! Let's develop a multipurpose building with a virtual component!"—the integrator either reels him in gently if he is still needed or sets him up on the next project. The integrator is the linchpin that holds everything together.

BUILDING A DREAM TEAM IS NOT EASY

The five personas we've described are by nature very strong-willed, and it's a challenge to get them to interact smoothly and move in the same direction. You will spend hours and hours in negotiation and debate, explaining everyone's different needs, arguing about customer pains, and so on. This may be painful, but don't give up! You will see progress—in fact, you will probably move forward more quickly than you thought possible. That's because the personas secure the future of the company. The innovator sparks the idea, the evangelist and the producer create the delight, and the administrator pays the taxes on time, controls inventory, and keeps the company on track. The integrator, meanwhile, runs back and forth, bridging gaps and making sure that the company, which currently looks like a lion, doesn't morph into a giraffe.

One last note: Sometimes a group might not seem to be exactly like the ideal team we've described here. If your group is small and the work is very people-centric, you may be tempted to allow individuals to take on more than one persona. That can work for a while, but only if those personas encompass that individual's strengths. Asking an individual to try to fulfill a role that preys on his or her weaknesses is simply a waste of time and resources. Instead, encourage all your team members to focus on their most effective personas and then bring complementary talent, attitude, and non-linear thinking to the table.

WHO'S ON YOUR TEAM?

YOU MIGHT HAVE A TEAM OR YOU MIGHT NOT! THE IMPORTANT QUESTION IS: DO YOU HAVE THE RIGHT TEAM?

Who is on the bus?

Who has already committed to joining you in your venture?

Why?

Why were they invited? Talents, connections, money, or other reasons?

YOUR FUTURE TEAM?

OK! YOU KNOW WHO AND WHY YOU BROUGHT THOSE PEOPLE ON BOARD THE BUS!
NEXT QUESTION IS: WHO ELSE DO YOU NEED ON THE BUS TO SUCCEED?

Who else to bring on board?

Where do you anticipate that you have gaps in your team?

Why?

What competence gaps do you need to close?

Who would need to get off the bus?

What players arrived early, but aren't pulling their weight?

CREATE YOUR TEAM

THE TEAM YOU NEED TO GET ON THE BUS–HOW DO THEY FIT INTO THE CUBE?

Name the person you plan to add to your team: _____

Non-LINEAR thinking–does this person have the ability to think beyond?

Inspiration: "Steve Jobs had the ability to create new markets and disrupt existing ones."

DELIVERY–can this person finish the job?

Inspiration: "This person always delivers on time and without too much guidance."

TALENT–how talented is this person?

Inspiration: "This person is the heavyweight champion of the world in her field."

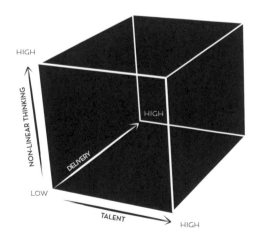

Note! *Fill your bus with the right people, or you are going nowhere.*

PERSONAS

THE THREE CORE ATTRIBUTES MENTIONED ON THE PREVIOUS PAGE CAN BE ENCOMPASSED INTO PERSONAS. A GOOD TEAM INCLUDES FIVE KEY PERSONAS.

Who on your team is the ...

Innovator:

Evangelist:

Producer:

Administrator:

Integrator:

WHY YOU ARE RIGHT

ARGUE FOR WHY YOU ARE THE RIGHT TEAM TO RELIEVE THE CUSTOMERS' PAIN.

Your competencies:

Inspiration: "We have 100 years of experience in surfing combined."

Your resources:

Inspiration: "We have great connections with the surfers' community in Santa Cruz. They really want to show our surfboard at the next competition. We have a friend who has made it in the IT world who wants to invest money."

Your passion:

Inspiration: "Surfing is our religion."

Note! *This is where you turn the idea from **an** opportunity to **your** opportunity!*

CHAPTER SUMMARY – TEAM

Getting the right people on the bus is not an easy thing, but since your team is your biggest asset, it's vital that you assemble a stellar group. Make sure you bring on board exceptionally talented, non-linear thinkers who can deliver. The innovator and the evangelist are usually the first personas on the team, but as soon as the business starts to grow, you will need to add the producer, the administrator, and the integrator. Before you go ahead and invite your dream team to join you on the journey, however, you should ask yourself a few questions. If your answer is NO for any of the questions below, you need to reassess your team!

QUESTIONS THAT REQUIRE AN ANSWER:

1 Do you have world-class talent on your team?
2 Are your team members non-linear thinkers who can deliver?
3 Have you made sure to include all five critical personas: the innovator, the evangelist, the producer, the administrator, and the integrator?

SYNC YOUR GEARS...SYNC YOUR TEAM

The best team will nail all the gears! Be sure you have the right team for your business opportunity.

REMEMBER

Fill your bus with the right people, or there's no point in going anywhere.

REALITY CHECK

ALWAYS FACE THE BRUTAL FACTS.

ONLY THE TRUTH SOUNDS LIKE THE TRUTH

⚙ REALITY CHECK

IN THIS LAST GEAR, THE HARD QUESTIONS HAVE TO BE ASKED: WILL THE IDEA REALLY WORK? HAVE THE GOOD, THE BAD, AND THE UGLY BEEN LAID OUT? IS THAT BEAUTIFUL UPWARD SLOPE IN THE PROFIT AND LOSS SHEET A REALITY? CAN ALL THE MOVING PARTS BE HANDLED? WILL A GLOBAL MARKET BE REACHED FROM THE GARAGE? HOW LIKELY IS IT THAT WALMART WILL BECOME A PARTNER? WHAT ARE THE ODDS THAT THE CREATION WILL FLY?

Doing a reality check is like interrogating your business opportunity to find out whether its plans are logical and realistic.

HIT WHERE IT HURTS: THE BRUTAL TRUTH

Why do you want to create this business? Money, fame, fortune, or just a burning desire to cure a pain that exists? The more important question is, are you prepared to take this idea all the way? And why should this idea make it? Most ideas don't! We salute all the dreamers out there, but let's be honest, the statistics are generally not in the entrepreneur's favor. What are the weak points and the strengths in the idea? What are the team's strengths? It is easy to get carried away when you're passionate about an idea, but passion isn't enough.

So let's get started!

IDENTIFY THE RISKS

Let's use the gears, go through the risks connected to them, and prepare. Identify at least one risk for each gear, then consider what you can do to prevent each one from happening.

yourself? "But a cool-looking iPad holder for the car is our delight," you say? That's probably not a sustainable delight. In fact, by the time your iPad holder is produced, your competitors have already had several of them on the market for months. So no delight there! Again, what is the delight? Will your customers tell their friends about your delight?

CUSTOMERS

Does the customer pain identified afflict anyone other than the closest circle of Family, Friends, and Fools? Too many times we hear people pitching ideas based on only their own needs or desires, but the idea needs to go further, there has to be a more widespread pain. Remember that statement from the customers gear: If you can ride with them, then you can sell to them. But if the pain is only for a few, there is no market, and then it is not a business but a hobby project.

DELIGHT

Do you really have a delight, or have you just added yet another function and are calling it delight? Are you fooling

CUSTOMER ACQUISITION

Once there is a strong delight in the product, consider how many potential customers there are. What is the unique sales formula, and what are the magic moves that will get more customers through the door in an innovative way?

BUSINESS MODEL

How will you make money? Do you have any zeros in your spreadsheet? Are there enough of them? It is not enough to be proud of how well costs have been lowered! Lowering costs only allows you to perform a little bit better on the cost side, but adding zeros truly reinvents the business model. More than one revenue stream? Is the pricing structure unique? (The world doesn't need one more freemium plan with ads!)

PARTNERS

Who are the right partners for the opportunity? Are they already onboard or are the existing partners just "good enough"? Be sure to be clear about not only what they can give but what they will get.

Let's suppose the plan is to have 150 new customers in 12 months. That means three new customers every week for a whole year! Do the math: 300 NEW leads per week, and initiate deeper and longer conversations with at least 30 of those leads, in order to get those three customers every week. It is one thing to invent delight, but it's a totally different thing to convince the world about it. Does the team have what it takes to get the job done? Remember: This cannot be outsourced to a call center or a recently-hired sales guy. The team has to do the selling until there is a unique sales formula; only then might others be able to do some of the work.

TEAM

Is there a world-class team that is suited to the opportunity? Why didn't they join the well-known companies in the industry instead? Are the people on the team the ones that just showed up for the ride, or are they world-class talent? Be honest about skills and ambitions. The big leagues require a different team, team members may have to be replaced—even the evangelist might have to look for another job. Why? Because it takes a different skill set to grow a company than to start it.

COMPETITORS

Get real! To be new to an existing market with an ambition to outperform is incredibly hard. Who will beat Oracle at its own game? Instead change the game and go in a direction that your competitors would never dream about. There might be a Blue Ocean to dive into.

GO GLOBAL

Is the business done in the parts of the world that will give the most leverage, or is the business done where it is most convenient? The Internet has no boundaries; it is only a lack of vision that limits an idea.

HIGH STAKES, NO PRISONERS

What are the biggest risks with the business idea and the execution? There have to be risks attached to any venture—no guts, no glory! First, identify the risks, then consider how to prevent the worst from happening. And figure out what to do if it does happen. It might also be wise to assess how likely it is that things will go wrong. Finally, assess how costly it would be for the venture if any of those things happened.

The facts can seem discouraging! Goals have to be stretched. It's OK to spend three years in stealth mode, provided that the risks were identified from the beginning. The worst thing that anyone can do is to announce that the product will hit the market in four months, and then take three years to develop it. Inevitably, the time will come when any company has to deliver the bad news: The prototype is taking longer to develop than planned, the manufacturing plant in Antarctica didn't deliver, the marketing guy is having a brain freeze, or the sales team is not closing any deals. It's OK; it will happen! Avoid presenting surprises. Be brutally honest, face the facts, plan for avoidance, and be ready when it happens.

BE PREPARED TO SHOULDER THE BLAME

Let's say you start an energy business with the idea of buying old Soviet nuclear submarines to generate electricity. You plan to install them in San Francisco Bay and start churning out electricity. While you've certainly earned high marks for creative thinking, an idea that far outside the box deserves a serious severity analysis before you start prototyping. Additional things to consider in a reality check:

1 Environmental Analysis

Try to identify key political, macroeconomic, regulatory, technological, and ecological forces that will influence the work with various markets and in different regions.

2 Ethical Analysis

An ethical analysis is simple. It is all about you! Are you comfortable conducting the business you're planning to run? Are there any moral implications for you and your team? If you feel at all uneasy with what you are proposing, go back and revise the content connected to the different gears. Make sure you can stand up tall and be proud of the business you are trying to launch.

RISK IN EACH GEAR

DEFINE THE RISK IN EACH GEAR. START WITH THE GEAR YOU BELIEVE HAS THE BIGGEST IMPACT ON YOUR BUSINESS.

Describe and define the risk in the gear _____ **(e.g., Competitors):**

Inspiration: "Your concept is being cloned by competitors."

How can you avoid it?

Inspiration: "Patents have to be filed. Trademarks need to be registered. Code needs to be protected."

What will you do if it happens?

Inspiration: "Investigate the opportunity to join your competitor and release a 2.0 of your product, even if it isn't ready."

Probability?

Inspiration: "Differentiate among Low, Medium, and High."

Severity?

Inspiration: "Differentiate among Low, Medium, and High."

Please, continue defining the risks for each gear on a separate piece of paper.

THE SUM OF ALL FEARS

IN ORDER OF IMPORTANCE, PLACE THE RISKS YOU HAVE IDENTIFIED IN THE CHART BELOW.

	THE RISK	HOW CAN YOU AVOID IT	WHAT WILL YOU DO IF IT HAPPENS?	PROBABILITY?	SEVERITY?
1	Loosing key employees	Stock option plan	Succession planning	15%	30%
2	Product banned by regulations	Lobbying	Close shop	1%	99%
3	Compelilion	Competition	Increase marketing	80%	15%
4	External funding	Boot strap	Boot strap	70%	0%
5	Product failure	Test sell, make a prototype	Buy competitor startup	5%	70%

START STOP KEEP

WHAT SHOULD YOU START DOING MORE OF, STOP DOING, AND KEEP ON DOING TO REACH YOUR GOALS FASTER?

	START DOING	STOP DOING	KEEP DOING
1	*More sales activities*	*Consultancy gigs (takes resources and energy)*	*Motivating team*
2			
3			
4			
5			

CHAPTER SUMMARY – REALITY CHECK

No one really likes spending time and energy on trying to define what's wrong with an idea, especially when everything is going well. We understand how frustrating it can be, but it has to be done! Spend resources on identifying potential risks and always keep an eye on the company dashboard to recognize when a change in course is needed. When things go wrong, the time between detection, action, and back on track will be shorter if you've spent time doing a reality check and are prepared for any problems that might arise.

THE LAST QUESTIONS, BUT PERHAPS THE MOST IMPORTANT ONES:

1   Have you done your math?
2   Do you know what can go wrong? Do you know how to avoid it?
3   What will you do if it happens?
4   How severe will it be for the company?
5   And what is the probability that it will happen?

SYNC YOUR GEARS...SYNC WITH REALITY TEST

Sync all the gears with a reality test! It can make a huge difference for how you can avoid and mitigate risks.

REMEMBER

Face the brutal facts, then act on them.

SYNC YOUR GEARS

GET IT ALL TO SPIN.

WAS IT HARD TO FIND THE EDGE IN EACH GEAR? OUR HOPE IS THAT YOU WILL GRASP THE BASICS OF THIS FRAMEWORK IN A SNAP, BUT THE TRUTH IS, BUSINESS IS HARD! IT WILL TAKE A LIFETIME TO MASTER. EVEN IF YOU ARE PRETTY COMFORTABLE UNDERSTANDING AND APPLYING THE CONCEPTS OF THE INDIVIDUAL GEARS, THERE IS STILL ONE CRUCIAL PART LEFT: TO SYNC THE GEARS AND MASTER THEM AS ONE UNIT.

Suppose you change the direction of one gear, or a gear gets stuck. Then your progress might be delayed or the project might be terminated. The next step, therefore, is to review the interactions between the gears and get all the gears working together like clockwork.

We have deliberately avoided giving too much direction on how to apply Gear Up, but we will conclude this book with a few suggestions that might help sync your gears and finish creating the unique customer acquisition-centric strategy for your business opportunity.

Remember, it's in the interaction between the different gears that a potential mismatch in your idea might be apparent. Go through the contact points described below, keep in mind your honest assessment from the Reality Check, and carefully review potential problems. Fix those problems, make any necessary changes, and review again. We can't emphasize enough the importance of this activity; paying attention to the interactions between the gears can make or break your business opportunity.

Let's go through a few of the gears' contact points to get you started. For your opportunity, you might need to review interactions between other gears. The challenge is to focus on the right interactions and use time and resources wisely.

IS THERE A PAIN FOR YOUR DELIGHT?

The first interaction to focus on is between customers' pain and delight: Do the target customers' pain and the solution create delight? If not, you need to either tweak the delight to fit the customers or modify your view of the target customers and their pain. As in real life, you will probably need to do a little bit of both.

SYNC YOUR SALES FORMULA

The gears delight—customer acquisition, and business model—are the centerpiece of your business-opportunity creation. When they're bundled together, we call them your unique sales formula. The reason these gears are at the center is plain and simple; even if there is a large potential customer base and the customers' pain is obvious, your idea might not lead to a profitable business unless you can get these three gears to spin as one, creating an effective sales formula.

Let's look at the overlapping areas between these central gears where obstructions might prevent them from spinning in sync. You can gain a lot, and save resources and time if you use delight as a way to keep customers loyal and get new customers. How can you include delight in the way you acquire and keep customers? How can you be sure customers will have smiles on their faces from their first contact with you all the way through using your product or service?

Too often, when developing a business opportunity, customer acquisition is seen as a separate activity from other activities in the company. In many companies, it is not until later (much too late!) that people with sales and market-ing expertise are added to the team, and even then it is often done with some grumbling from the founders and the engineers. That is not a smart way of developing a business opportunity! Customer acquisition should be an integral part of how the business is going to make money and reduce cost. Acquiring customers is a part of the company's delight. No customers, no revenue, no fun.

There are a lot of ways to utilize delight in a business model. Think about what could improve the experience for customers while also making more money or reducing costs. One suggestion is to strip the offering of everything that is not clearly contributing to the pyramid of functionality, efficiency, and delight. Question every piece of your offering: "Does this increase the value of our product or service?"

Now it's time to go further and sync all of the gears. As you go forward, treat the three sales formula gears—delight, customer acquisition, and business model—as one single gear. If, for one reason or another, you realize along the way that your sales formula is not synced, then you'll have to go back, unbundle the three, and sync them again.

SYNCING YOUR GEARS

PREVIOUSLY WE HAVE FOCUSED ON MAXIMIZING PERFORMANCE IN EACH GEAR. NOW IT'S TIME TO MAXIMIZE OVERALL PERFORMANCE AND GET THE GEARS TO WORK TOGETHER. IF ONE GEAR IS STUCK, IT CAN JEOPARDIZE THE WHOLE BUSINESS. HOW CAN YOU SYNC YOUR GEARS TO GET THEM ALL TO SPIN FASTER?

Customer Acquisition and Team: do they sync?

Inspiration: "You have a team that is skillfull in technology, but inexperienced in aquiring customers for your business."

How can you solve this problem?

Inspiration: "Google: Sales is math. "I can make a better sales guy out of a technician than a technician out of a sales guy. Good sales is built into the product."

Business Model and Customer Acquisition— do they sync?

Inspiration: "A high price could dramatically increase the cost of customer acquisition."

How can you solve this problem?

Inspiration: "A cable TV company changed from a high fixed price to a monthly subscription. That lowered the customer acquisition cost and increased total revenue from the customers."

IS YOUR UNIQUE SALES FORMULA MADE EVEN MORE UNIQUE BY YOUR WAY OF WORKING WITH PARTNERS?

Good partners are worth striving for. Realizing how partners can contribute to the sales formula can lead to a real breakthrough in the opportunity assessment. Challenge yourself and your partners and think about how they can help make the sales formula even more unique: Can they include your offering in their sales, contributing to your customer acquisition? Can you join your delight with theirs so the value of both offerings increases? Can you add more zeros to your spreadsheet by increasing interaction with your partners? Can you add revenue to both your bottom line and theirs by aligning your business models?

There is no point in moving forward with the rest of the gears if you are not sure about the alignment of the gears we have touched upon so far. You might be able to kid yourself and your team for now, but if you haven't done this right, reality will hit when you go to execute your business opportunity.

When you're ready, keep on reading!

(Don't try to cheat by moving on too quickly.)

ARE YOU READY TO GO GLOBAL?

Maybe you have already decided that you don't want to go global, and that's fine! In our experience, when we see companies hesitating to go global, it's most often because their existing sales formula is not globally competitive, or because they still need to prove they can actually solve a customer pain with their solution.

If you truly don't want to go global, then you can skip this sync and move to the last gear. But if you are sure you want to go global or have even a slight urge to do so, then the synchronization of this gear with all the previous ones is extremely important. You might have everything right so far, but before you take it to a global level, everything (and we mean everything!) you have done so far has to be tested

again based on your global vision. You'll need to start from the very beginning of the chapter and go through each gear again (if you have done a thorough job thus far, it should not be that painful). There are no shortcuts, though, so let's do it all over again—this time with the whole world in mind! Great! Now you not only have a unique sales formula, but you have gone one step further to create a unique global sales formula. With that in place, you have the whole world at your feet. Cool!

You know what comes next ...

SPIN THE GEARS!

By now you should have a pretty good sense of what interactions between the gears you need to focus on. Go on, go back, move forward, and don't hesitate to take a leap of faith. Don't back off from the areas where you know there are challenges and hurdles—it builds character and will make your business opportunities that much stronger.

TAKE ACTION

You've done as much as you can alone in your dorm, garage, or office. Luck will not come to you; you have to go out and make yourself lucky. You have your unique customer acquisition-centric strategy. That, together with your passion for curing your customers' pain, is what will move you forward. It is your responsibility to act on what you have created. No one else will do it for you, but hopefully you've found several people who will do it with you.

MAKE MISTAKES

There is rarely a perfect solution or strategy that hits the bull's-eye in just one shot. As you take action, expect to make mistakes. The best business strategies are a conglomeration of mistakes made and lessons learned from interactions with customers, partners, competitors, team members, and so on. Thomas Edison once said, "Many of life's failures are people who did not realize how close they were to success when they gave up."

CELEBRATE SUCCESS

Too often we avoid appreciating our successes, but it's much better to celebrate every success—even the small ones—along the way. Don't worry; shouting "hooray!" will not jinx you! It won't prevent your next mistake, either (because there will always be mistakes), but a positive attitude will lead to even more success in the future.

THERE IS NO END

Taking a business from an idea to a successful company is a long journey with no clear destination. The art of business is fine-tuning all nine gears and constantly iterating. Your Plan A might soon be forgotten as you change it multiple times; by the time you launch it might be more like Plan G. Many of today's most successful companies did not get it right the first time. Instead it took multiple small failures and mistakes to get it right. To be successful you have to make mistakes—and learn from them.

Successful entrepreneurs and executives are able to understand and solve challenges in all the gears and get them to sync. They have a clear passion for curing their customers' pain, and they move from gear to gear to create the best overall solution. We have watched many companies, entrepreneurs, and executives fail because they place too much emphasis on one gear. Being the best in only one gear is not good enough! You have to excel in all nine—at the same time.

In the end, business is all about winning, and we hope that Gear Up will help you win.

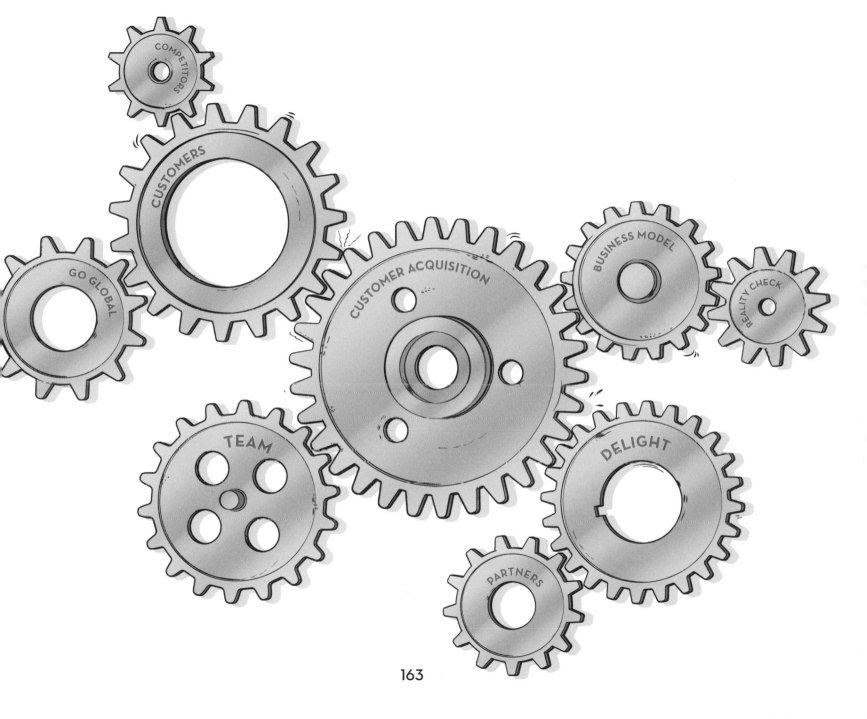

CHALLENGE: SYNC ALL THE GEARS

MOST FUNDAMENTAL IS TO GET ALL THE GEARS TO MOVE IN THE RIGHT DIRECTION. BUSINESS IS A HARD GAME. YOU MIGHT THINK YOU KNOW ALL ABOUT THE GEARS, BUT SYNCING THEM CAN TAKE A LIFETIME TO MASTER. SUPPOSE YOU CHANGE THE DIRECTION OF ONE GEAR; THEN YOUR PROGRESS MIGHT GET DELAYED OR TERMINATED.

WHERE DO YOU FIND MOST FRICTION? AND WHAT GEARS WORK GREAT TOGETHER?

Mark the boxes where gears work perfectly with: ✔

Mark the boxes where there is a challenge with: ✘

If ✘ , go back to the chapter and redo the work
so that friction is removed.

			CUSTOMER ACQUIS⌐ BUSINESS MODE⌐
		DELIGHT/ CUSTOMER ACQUISITION	DELIGHT/ BUSINESS MODE⌐
	CUSTOMERS/ DELIGHT	CUSTOMERS/ CUSTOMER ACQUISITION	CUSTOMERS/ BUSINESS MODE⌐

CUSTOMERS   **DELIGHT**   **CUSTOMER ACQUISITION**   **BUSINESS MODE**

	PARTNERS	COMPETITORS	GO GLOBAL	TEAM	REALITY CHECK
					TEAM / REALITY CHECK
				GO GLOBAL / TEAM	GO GLOBAL / REALITY CHECK
			COMPETITORS / GO GLOBAL	COMPETITORS / TEAM	COMPETITORS / REALITY CHECK
		PARTNERS / COMPETITORS	PARTNERS / GO GLOBAL	PARTNERS / TEAM	PARTNERS /REALITY CHECK
	BUSINESS MODEL/ PARTNERS	BUSINESS MODEL / COMPETITORS	BUSINESS MODEL / GO GLOBAL	BUSINESS MODEL / TEAM	BUSINESS MODEL / REALITY CHECK
	CUSTOMER ACQUISITION/ PARTNERS	CUSTOMER ACQUISITION/ COMPETITORS	CUSTOMER ACQUISITION/ GO GLOBAL	CUSTOMER ACQUISITION/ TEAM	CUSTOMER ACQUISITION/ REALITY CHECK
	DELIGHT/ PARTNERS	DELIGHT / COMPETITORS	DELIGHT / GO GLOBAL	DELIGHT / TEAM	DELIGHT / REALITY CHECK
	CUSTOMERS/ PARTNERS	CUSTOMERS / COMPETITORS	CUSTOMERS / GO GLOBAL	CUSTOMERS / TEAM	CUSTOMERS / REALITY CHECK

PARTNERS   **COMPETITORS**   **GO GLOBAL**   **TEAM**   **REALITY CHECK**

YOU DON'T HAVE TO TRUST US

DIG DEEP INTO THE SOURCES.

Top shelf

THE NUDIST ON THE LATE SHIFT

GETTING PAST NO

THE TROPHY KIDS GROW UP

COMPETING FOR THE FUTURE

Hidden in Plain Sight

INFLUENCE: THE PSYCHOLOGY OF PERSURSION

INFLUENCE: SCIENCE AND PRACTICE

GOOD TO GREAT

LEARNED OPTIMISM

Getting to Plan B

THE ART OF THE START

Middle shelf

BUSINESS STRIPPED BARE

CROSSING THE CHASM

FINDING GREAT IDEAS IN EMERGING MARKETS

WOMEN WANT MORE

Fuzzy logic: Cartoons

Reality Check

Shaking Things Up at Coca-Cola

BLUE OCEAN STRATEGY

The New Business Road Test

Inside the Tornado

The Insicle Story of Intrigue

Bottom shelf

DEALING WITH DARWIN

The Case of Multitasking

Finding Great Ideas in Emerging Markets

NOTHING'S IMPOSSIBLE

lonely planet
SOUTH PACIFIC & MICRONESIA

BUILT TO LAST

Cult of iPod

Positioning: The Battle for Your Mind

The Kama Sutra

Why Most Product Launches Fail

Living on the Faults Line

merry x-mas

THE PEOPLE ON THE BUS

TOM KOSNIK

Tom Kosnik is a Professor at Stanford University. Tom started his teaching journey at Harvard, where he laid the foundation for this book by initiating work with the DDART framework – Diagnose, Decision, Analysis, and Reality Test. DDART was developed after many years of research with the goal to help students, entrepreneurs, and businesses decipher new and existing business opportunities.

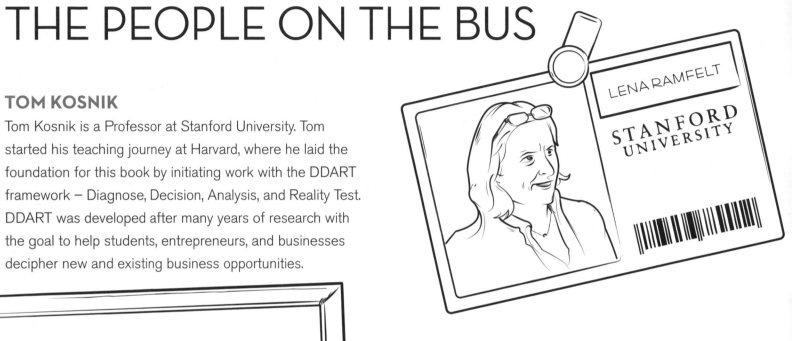

TOM KOSNIK

LENA RAMFELT

Lena Ramfelt holds a PhD from Stockholm University. She joined forces with Tom at Stanford and the two of them have been teaching together since 1997. During their years together, they have seen Silicon Valley grow and outperform the rest of the world in building new large and successful companies. Together they interviewed, explored, and captured information on these growing companies. This newfound insight was mixed with existing knowledge and taught to students together with what the most successful entrepreneurs in Silicon Valley had to offer. One company Lena studied was Skype, which was how Tom and Lena met Jonas.

JONAS KJELLBERG

Jonas Kjellberg, a serial entrepreneur and venture capitalist, was a member of the Skype leadership team when he met Tom and Lena. Jonas had started a handful of companies and invested in even more. Jonas started to lecture in Tom's and Lena's marketing classes about the real life of building companies, the challenges and the gains, and what kind of thinking it took to build Skype. Jonas and Lena started to compare notes on what kind of innovative thinking was needed for success, but more importantly, why some good ideas and companies made it while others didn't.
Jonas had a vision to take lessons learned from hyper-growth companies, combine those lessons with what was taught at world-class universities, revamp it to create a user-friendly version, and make it accessible to entrepreneurs around the world. Tom, Lena, and Jonas became a great team. Their combination of academic knowledge and real-life experience is the foundation for this book.

With Tom as a mentor, Jonas and Lena set out on a journey to write *Gear Up: Bring Business Opportunities to Life*.

The challenge was to get it academically correct, base it on real-life entrepreneurship, and get the job done, yet still make it accessible for everyone interested in the subject. The team's ambition was to capture the best theories from the most inspiring authors and add their own research and experiences.

... THE CREATIVE GUYS, ULF AND JOHAN

This book would not exist without all the time and energy put in by Ulf Öman, the creative director and producer. This book would not be what it is without the incredible illustrator Johan Röstwall, who had the challenge of illustrating the ideas. Each of his illustrations says more than a thousand words.

AND THE WORDING

Without the help of Lilith Z.C. Fondulas, this book would still be in beta. Today Lilith is an editor for The Boston Consulting Group. Prior to joining BCG, Lilith edited books and articles, especially for Harvard Business Review.

THE JOURNEY

The journey has been both interesting and rewarding. The next challenge is to create a Digital Learning Tool so readers can formulate and communicate their own unique customer acquisition-centric strategies, learn more, and also share stories and advice with each other. The team has also started working on developing "Deep Dives," which are separate books for every gear where more experiences, and more in-depth descriptions of the particular gears, will be presented with more tools and examples from companies and enterprises. Whether this book has changed the game for management literature is still to be proven. This journey is built on constant communication with existing and potential customers. The interaction and the feedback have been extraordinary; everything from spelling mistakes to shortcomings in content have been corrected thanks to this interaction. New material has been included, obsolete content cut, and not-so-good illustrations have been improved. This point has been reached because of a lot of interactions with potential customers.

ULF ÖMAN

LILITH Z.C. FONDULAS

JOHAN RÖSTWALL

YOU'VE READ THIS FAR, DON'T STOP NOW! PICK A FEW BOOKS AND ARTICLES FROM THIS LIST TO READ AND SEE HOW THE IDEAS PRESENTED CAN CONTRIBUTE TO YOUR OWN SUCCESS. WE BET YOU WILL HAVE A LOT OF FUN READING THEM, TOO!

CUSTOMERS

"Can't ride with them. Can't sell to them." From a conversation Jonas had in a Harley-Davidson shop in California.

"Reason to be." Quote by Lars Johan Jarnheimer, board member IKEA, SAS and former CEO at Tele2.

Alsop, Ron. The Trophy Kids Grow Up: How the Millennial Generation is Shaking Up the Workplace. US: Jossey-Bass, 2008.

Anderson, Chris. The Long Tail, Revised and Updated Edition: Why the Future of Business is Selling Less of More. US: Hyperion, 2008.

Blank, Steven Gary. The Four Steps to the Epiphany. US: Cafepress.com, 2005.

Cool, Karen and Petros Paranikas. "When Every Customer Is a New Customer." Harvard Business Review 89 (May 2011): 29-31.

Grimes, John. Reality Check. US: Ten Speed Press, 1993.

Grimes, John. Fuzzy logic: Cartoons. US: J. Grimes, 1998.

Joachimsthaler, Erich. Hidden in Plain Sight: How to Find and Execute Your Company's Next Big Growth Strategy. US: Harvard Business School Publishing, 2007.

Kahney, Leander. Cult of iPod. US: No Starch Press, 2005.

Maslow, A.H. Maslow on Management. US: Wiley, 1998.

Moore, Geoffrey A. Inside the Tornado: Marketing Strategies from Silicon Valley's Cutting Edge. US: HarperBusiness, 1999.

Moore, Geoffrey A. Crossing the Chasm. US: Harper Paperbacks, 2002.

Moore, Geoffrey A. Living on the Fault Line, Revised Edition: Managing for Shareholder Value in Any Economy. US: HarperBusiness, 2002.

Moore, Geoffrey A. Dealing with Darwin: How Great Companies Innovate at Every Phase of Their Evolution. US: Portfolio Hardcover, 2005.

Mullins, John. The New Business Road Test: What entrepreneurs and executives should do before writing a business plan. US: FT Press, 2004.

Schneider, Joan and Julie Hall "Why Most Product Launches Fail." Harvard Business Review 89 (April 2011): 21-23.

Silverstein, Michael J., Kate Sayre, and John Butman. Women Want More: How to Capture Your Share of the World's Largest, Fastest-Growing Market. US: HarperBusiness, 2009.

Simester Duncan. "When You Shouldn't Listen to Your Critics." Harvard Business Review 89 (June 2011): 42.

Washburn Nathan T., and B. Tom Hunsaker. "Finding Great Ideas in Emerging Markets." Harvard Business Review 89 (September 2011): 115-120.

A classic!

Read before writing a business plan

...en in loop!

⚙ SOURCES

DELIGHT

"Innovate, don't imitate." Inspiration from Nordstrom, Kjell, A. Karaoke Capitalism. Management for Mankind. Sweden: Bookhouse Publishing AB, 2003.

Brown, Bruce, and Scott, D. Anthony. "How P&G Tripled Its Innovation Success Rate." Harvard Business Review 89 (June 2011): 64-72.

Frank, Milo O. How to Get Your Point Across in 30 Seconds or Less. US: Pocket, 1990.

Gladwell, Malcolm. The Tipping Point: How Little Things Can Make a Big Difference. US: Back Bay Books, 2002.

Godin, Seth. All Marketers Are Liars: The Power of Telling Authentic Stories in a Low-Trust World. US: Portfolio Hardcover, 2005.

Grimes, John. Reality Check. US: Ten Speed Press, 1993.

Grimes, John. Fuzzy logic: Cartoons. US: J. Grimes, 1998.

Hughes, Mark. Buzzmarketing: Get People to Talk About Your Stuff. US: Portfolio Trade, 2008.

Joachimsthaler, Erich. Hidden in Plain Sight: How to Find and Execute Your Company's Next Big Growth Strategy. US: Harvard Business School Publishing, 2007.

Kahney, Leander. Cult of iPod. US: No Starch Press, 2005.

Kawasaki, Guy. The Art of the Start: The Time-Tested, Battle-Hardened Guide for Anyone Starting Anything. US: Portfolio Hardcover, 2004.

Kawasaki, Guy. Reality Check: The Irreverent Guide to Outsmarting, Outmanaging, and Outmarketing Your Competition. US: Portfolio Hardcover, 2008.

Kawasaki, Guy. Enchantment: The Art of Changing Hearts, Minds, and Actions. US: Portfolio Hardcover, 2011.

Keiningham, Timothy, L., Aksoy, Lerzan, Buoye, Alexander and Bruce Cooil Washburn. "Customer Loyalty Isn't Enough. Grow Your Share of Wallet." Harvard Business Review 89 (October 2011): 29-31.

Kent, Muhtar and Adi Ignatius. "Shaking Things Up at Coca-Cola." Harvard Business Review 89 (October 2011): 94-99.

Kourdi, Jeremy. 100 Great Business Ideas: From Leading Companies Around the World. US: Marshall Cavendish Corp/Ccb, 2010.

Lewis, Michael. The Future Just Happened. US: Coronet Books, 2002.

Martin, Roger, L. "The Innovation Catalysts." Harvard Business Review 89 (June 2011): 82-87.

Monroe, Lorraine. Nothing's Impossible: Leadership Lessons From Inside And Outside The Classroom. US: PublicAffairs, 1999.

Ries, Al, and Jack Trout. Positioning: The Battle for Your Mind. US: McGraw-Hill, 2000.

Schmitt, Philipp, Skiers, Bernard, and Christophe Van den Bulte. "Why Customer Referrals Can Drive Stunning Profits." Harvard Business Review 89 (June 2011): 30.

Silverstein, Michael J., Kate Sayre, and John Butman. Women Want More: How to Capture Your Share of the World's Largest, Fastest-Growing Market. US: HarperBusiness, 2009.

Wiefels, Paul. The Chasm Companion: Implementing Effective Marketing Strategies for High-Technology Companies. US: Harper Paperbacks, 2002.

CUSTOMER ACQUISITION

"Always be closing." From the movie "Glengary Glen Ross," 1992.

Frequency in your product!

Aral, Sinan, and Dylan Walker. "Forget Viral Marketing-Make the Product Itself Viral." Harvard Business Review 89 (June 2011): 34-35.

Grimes, John. Reality Check. US: Ten Speed Press, 1993.

Grimes, John. Fuzzy logic: Cartoons. US: J. Grimes, 1998.

Kawasaki, Guy. Reality Check: The Irreverent Guide to Outsmarting, Outmanaging, and Outmarketing Your Competition. US: Portfolio Hardcover, 2008.

Li, Charlene, and Josh Bernoff. Groundswell: Winning in a World Transformed by Social Technologies. US: Harvard Business Press, 2008.

Li, Charlene. Open Leadership: How Social Technology Can Transform the Way You Lead. US: Jossey-Bass, 2010.

Ries, Al, and Jack Trout. Positioning: The Battle for Your Mind. US: McGraw-Hill, 2000.

Rogers, Everett M., and Everett Rogers. Diffusion of Innovations, 5th Edition. New York: Free Press, 2003.

Schiffman, Stephan. Getting to Closed: A Proven Program to Accelerate the Sales Cycle and Increase Commissions. US: Dearborn Trade Publishing, 2002.

Schiffman, Stephan. Cold Calling Techniques (That Really Work!). US: Adams Media, 2007.

Schiffman, Stephan. The 25 Sales Habits of Highly Successful Salespeople. US: Adams Media, 2008.

Shih, Clara. The Facebook Era: Tapping Online Social Networks to Build Better Products, Reach New Audiences, and Sell More Stuff. US: Prentice Hall, 2009.

Silverstein, Michael J., Kate Sayre, and John Butman. Women Want More: How to Capture Your Share of the World's Largest, Fastest-Growing Market. US: HarperBusiness, 2009.

Tannen, Deborah. Talking From 9 to 5: Women and Men in the Workplace: Language, Sex, and Power. New York, NY: William Morrow, and Company, 1994.

Wiefels, Paul. The Chasm Companion: Implementing Effective Marketing Strategies for High-Technology Companies. US: Harper Paperbacks, 2002.

Great tools!

BUSINESS MODEL

"From idea to cash." Our own contribution.

Anderson, Chris. Free: The Future of a Radical Price. US: Hyperion, 2009.

Byers, Thomas, Richard Dorf, and Andrew Nelson. Technology Ventures: From Idea to Enterprise. US: McGraw-Hill Science/Engineering/Math, 2010.

Bryce, David, J, Jeffrey H. Dyer, and Nile W. Hatch. "Competing Against Free." Harvard Business Review 89 (June 2011): 104-111.

Geirland, John, and Eva Sonesh-Keder. Digital Babylon: How the Geeks, the Suits, and the Ponytails Fought to Bring Hollywood to the Internet. US: Arcade Publishing, 1999.

SOURCES

Girotra, Karan, and Serguei Netessine. "How to Build Risk into Your Business Model." Harvard Business Review 89 (May 2011): 100-105.

Grimes, John. Reality Check. US: Ten Speed Press, 1993.

Grimes, John. Fuzzy logic: Cartoons. US: J. Grimes, 1998.

Mullins, John, and Randy Komisar. Getting to Plan B: Breaking Through to a Better Business Model. US: Harvard Business Press, 2009.

Nunes, Paul and Time Breene. "Reinvent Your Business Before it's too Late." Harvard Business Review 89 (January/February 2011): 80-87.

Omidyar, Pierre. "EBay's Founder on Innovating the Business Model of Social Change." Harvard Business Review 89 (September 2011): 41-44.

Osterwalder, Alexander, and Yves Pigneur. Business Model Generation: A Handbook for Visionaries, Game Changers, and Challengers. US: Wiley, 2010.

Prahalad, C.K. The Fortune at the Bottom of the Pyramid: Eradicating Poverty Through Profits. US: Wharton School Publishing, 2004.

Rangan, V. Kasturi, Michael Chu, and Djordjija Petkoski. "Segmenting the Base of the Pyramid." Harvard Business Review 89 (June 2011): 113-117.

Insightful!

Staats, Bradley, R. and David M. Upton. "Lean Knowledge Work." Harvard Business Review 89 (October 2011): 101-108.

PARTNERS

"Who loves you? Who hates you?"
Our own contribution.

Carlton, Jim. Apple: The Inside Story of Intrigue, Egomania, and Business Blunders. US: Crown Business, 1997.

Cialdini, Robert B. Influence: Science and Practice. US: Allyn & Bacon, 2000.

Cialdini, Robert B. Influence: The Psychology of Persuasion. US: Harper Paperbacks, 2006.

Fisher, Roger, William L. Ury, and Bruce Patton. Getting to Yes: Negotiating Agreement Without Giving In. US: Penguin (Non-Classics), 2011.

Grimes, John. Reality Check. US: Ten Speed Press, 1993.

Grimes, John. Fuzzy logic: Cartoons. US: J. Grimes, 1998.

Kawasaki, Guy. The Art of the Start: The Time-Tested, Battle-Hardened Guide for Anyone Starting Anything. US: Portfolio Hardcover, 2004.

Kawasaki, Guy. Reality Check: The Irreverent Guide to Outsmarting, Outmanaging, and Outmarketing Your Competition. US: Portfolio Hardcover, 2008.

Lebret, Herve. Start-Up: What We May Still Learn From Silicon Valley. US: CreateSpace, 2007.

Lewis, Michael. The New New Thing. New York, NY: W.W. Norton & Company, 1999.

Li, Charlene. Open Leadership: How Social Technology Can Transform the Way You Lead. US: Jossey-Bass, 2010.

Monroe, Lorraine. Nothing's Impossible: Leadership Lessons From Inside And Outside The Classroom. US: PublicAffairs, 1999.

Ury, William. Getting Past No. New York: Bantam, 1992.

Before you negotiate!

Ury, William. The Power of a Positive No: Save The Deal Save The Relationship and Still Say No. New York: Bantam, 2007.

Wiefels, Paul. The Chasm Companion: Implementing Effective Marketing Strategies for High-Technology Companies. US: Harper Paperbacks, 2002.

COMPETITORS

"Big Beats the Small or Fast Beats the Slow." Inspiration from Jan Stenbeck

Berger, Jonah, and Scott Berinato. "If You Want to Win, Tell Your Team It's Losing (a Little)." Harvard Business Review 89 (October 2011): 36-37.

Brown, Shona L., and Kathleen M. Eisenhardt. Competing on the Edge: Strategy as Structured Chaos. US: Harvard Business Press, 1998.

Christensen, Clayton M. The Innovator's Dilemma: When New Technologies Cause Great Firms to Fail. US: Harvard Business Press, 1997.

Christensen, Clayton M., and Michael E. Raynor. The Innovator's Solution: Creating and Sustaining Successful Growth. US:

A new per-
spective on
competition!

Harvard Business Press, 2003.

Elkington, John, and Pamela Hartigan. The Power of Unreasonable People: How Social Entrepreneurs Create Markets That Change the World. US: Harvard Business Press, 2008.

Grimes, John. Reality Check. US: Ten Speed Press, 1993.

Grimes, John. Fuzzy logic: Cartoons. US: J. Grimes, 1998.

Hamel, Gary, and C. K. Prahalad. Competing for the Future. US: Harvard Business Press, 1996.

Joachimsthaler, Erich. Hidden in Plain Sight: How to Find and Execute Your Company's Next Big Growth Strategy. US: Harvard Business School Publishing, 2007.

Kawasaki, Guy. Reality Check: The Irreverent Guide to Outsmarting, Outmanaging, and Outmarketing Your Competition. US: Portfolio Hardcover, 2008.

Keiningham, Timothy, L., Aksoy, Lerzan, Buoye, Alexander and Bruce Cooil Washburn. "Customer Loyalty Isn't Enough. Grow Your Share of Wallet." Harvard Business Review 89 (October 2011): 29-31.

Kim, W. Chan, and Renée Mauborgne. Blue Ocean Strategy: How to Create Uncontested Market Space and Make Competition Irrelevant. US: Harvard Business Press, 2004.

If you don't read anything else, read this one!

Kim, W. Chan, and Renée Mauborgne. "Blue Ocean Strategy." Harvard Business Review 82 (October 2004): 76-85.

Moore, Geoffrey A. Dealing with Darwin: How Great Companies Innovate at Every Phase of Their Evolution. US: Portfolio Hardcover, 2005.

Reeves, Martin, and Mike Deimler. "Adaptability: The New Competitive Advantage." Harvard Business Review 89 (July/August 2011): 135-141.

Zook, Chris. Beyond the Core: Expand Your Market Without Abandoning Your Roots. US: Harvard Business Press, 2004.

GO GLOBAL

"Good Ideas Have no Boundaries." Inspiration from Friedman, Thomas L., in The New York Times, October 6, 2006

Altman, Daniel. Connected: 24 Hours in the Global Economy. US: MacMillan, 2007.

SOURCES

Castells, Manuel. Technopoles of the World: The Making of 21st Century Industrial Complexes. US: Routledge, 1994.

Cole, Geert. Lonely Planet South Pacific & Micronesia. US: Lonely Planet, 2006.

Doz, Yves L., Jose Santos, and Peter Williamson. From Global to Metanational: How Companies Win in the Knowledge Economy. US: Harvard Business Press, 2001.

Friedman, Thomas L. The World Is Flat 3.0: A Brief History of the Twenty-first Century. US: Picador, 2007.

Friedman, Thomas L. Hot, Flat, and Crowded: Why We Need a Green Revolution—and How It Can Renew America. US: Farrar, Straus and Giroux, 2008.

Grimes, John. Reality Check. US: Ten Speed Press, 1993.

Grimes, John. Fuzzy logic: Cartoons. US: J. Grimes, 1998.

Hofstede, Geert, Gert Jan Hofstede, and Michael Minkov. Cultures and Organizations: Software for the Mind, Third Edition. US: McGraw-Hill, 2010.

Johnson, Bill. "The CEO of Heinz on Powering Growth in Emerging Markets."
Harvard Business Review 89 (October 2011): 47-50.

Kumar, Nirmalya and Phanish Puranam. "Have You Restructured for Global Success?" Harvard Business Review 89 (October 2011): 123-128.

Lipnack, Jessica, and Jeffrey Stamps. Virtual Teams: People Working Across Boundaries with Technology. US: Wiley, 2000.

McKendrick, David, Richard Doner, and Stephan Haggard. From Silicon Valley to Singapore: Location and Competitive Advantage in the Hard Disk Drive Industry. US: Stanford Business Books, 2000.

Nisbett, Richard. The Geography of Thought: How Asians and Westerners Think Differently...and Why. US: Free Press, 2003.

Popkin, James M., and Partha Iyengar. IT And the East: How China And India Are Altering the Future of Technology And Innovation. US: Harvard Business Press, 2007.

Prahalad, C.K. The Fortune at the Bottom of the Pyramid: Eradicating Poverty Through Profits. US: Wharton School Publishing, 2004.

Saxenian, AnnaLee. Regional Advantage: Culture and Competition in Silicon Valley and Route 128. US: Harvard University Press, 1996.

Saxenian, AnnaLee. The New Argonauts: Regional Advantage in a Global Economy. US: Harvard University Press, 2006.

Scott, Allen J. Regions and the World Economy: The Coming Shape of Global Production, Competition, and Political Order. US: Oxford University Press, 2000.

Trompenaars, Fons and Charles Hampden-Turner. Riding the Waves of Culture: Understanding Cultural Diversity in Business, Second Edition. New York, NY: McGraw Hill, 1998.

Washburn Nathan T., and B. Tom Hunsaker. "Finding Great Ideas in Emerging Markets." Harvard Business Review 89 (September 2011): 115-120.

TEAM

"Get the Right People on the Bus."
Collins, Jim. Good to Great: Why Some Companies Make the Leap...And Others Don't. US: HarperBusiness, 2001.

Incredible business opportunity here!

Berger, Jonah, and Scott Berinato. "If You Want to Win, Tell Your Team It's Losing (a Little)." Harvard Business Review 89 (October 2011): 36-37.

Branson, Richard. Business Stripped Bare. US: Virgin Books, 2009.

Bronson, Po. The Nudist on the Late Shift: And Other True Tales of Silicon Valley. US: Random House, 1999.

Carlton, Jim. Apple: The Inside Story of Intrigue, Egomania, and Business Blunders. US: Crown Business, 1997.

Carroll, Michael. The Mindful Leader: Awakening Your Natural Management Skills Through Mindfulness Meditation. US: Trumpeter, 2008.

Cialdini, Robert B. Influence: Science and Practice. US: Allyn & Bacon, 2000.

Cialdini, Robert B. Influence: The Psychology of Persuasion. US: Harper Paperbacks, 2006.

Collins, James C., and Jerry I. Porras. Built to Last. US: Harper Business, 1996.

Collins, Jim. Good to Great: Why Some Companies Make the Leap … And Others Don't. US: Harper Business, 2001.

Collins, Jim. How The Mighty Fall: And Why Some Companies Never Give In. US: Jim Collins, 2009.

Collins, Jim and Hansen, Morten, T. Great By Choice. US: HarperCollins books, 2011.

Coppola, Francis, Ford and Alison Beard. "Life's Work: Francis Ford Coppola." Harvard Business Review 89 (October 2011): 156.

Covey, Stephen R. The 7 Habits of Highly Effective People. US: Free Press, 2004.

DeMarco, Tom, and Timothy Lister. Peopleware: Productive Projects and Teams. US: Dorset House, 1999.

Elkington, John, and Pamela Hartigan. The Power of Unreasonable People: How Social Entrepreneurs Create Markets That Change the World. US: Harvard Business Press, 2008.

Fernandez-Araoz, Groysberg, Boris and Nitin Nohria. "How to Hang on to Your High Potentials." Harvard Business Review 89 (October 2011): 76-83.

Fisher, Roger, William L. Ury, and Bruce Patton. Getting to Yes: Negotiating Agreement Without Giving In. US: Penguin (Non-Classics), 2011.

Gardner, Howard. Five Minds for the Future. US: Harvard Business Press, 2007.

Grimes, John. Reality Check. US: Ten Speed Press, 1993.

Grimes, John. Fuzzy logic: Cartoons. US: J. Grimes, 1998.

Groysberg, Boris, L. Kevin, Kelly and Bryan, MacDonald. "The new path to the C-Suite." Harvard Business Review 89 (March 2011): 60-68.

Kanter, Rosabeth, Moss. "The Cure for Horrible Bosses." Harvard Business Review 89 (October 2011): 42.

Katzenbach, Jon R. and Douglas K. Smith. The Discipline of Teams. New York, NY: John Wiley & Sons, 2001.

Kawasaki, Guy. The Art of the Start: The Time-Tested, Battle-Hardened Guide for Anyone Starting Anything. US: Portfolio Hardcover, 2004.

Kawasaki, Guy. Reality Check: The Irreverent Guide to Outsmarting, Outmanaging, and Outmarketing Your Competition. US: Portfolio Hardcover, 2008.

Kennedy, John Fitzgerald. Profiles in Courage. US: Perennial, 2000.

:-)

Excellent reading!

Good advice!

SOURCES

Komisar, Randy, and Kent L. Lineback. The Monk and the Riddle: The Education of a Silicon Valley Entrepreneur. US: Harvard Business Press, 2000.

Kouzes, James M., and Barry Z. Posner. The Leadership Challenge, 4th Edition. CA: Jossey-Bass, 2008.

Lebret, Herve. Start-Up: What We May Still Learn From Silicon Valley. US: CreateSpace, 2007.

Lencioni, Patrick. The Five Dysfunctions of a Team. San Francisco, CA: Jossey-Bass, 2002.

Li, Charlene. Open Leadership: How Social Technology Can Transform the Way You Lead. US: Jossey-Bass, 2010.

Lipnack, Jessica, and Jeffrey Stamps. Virtual Teams: People Working Across Boundaries with Technology. US: Wiley, 2000.

Loehr, Jim, and Tony Schwartz. The Power Of Full Engagement: Managing Energy, Not Time, Is The Key To High Performance and Personal Renewal. NY: Free Pr, 2002.

Malone, Michael S. Betting It All: The Entrepreneurs of Technology. US: Wiley, 2001.

Monroe, Lorraine. Nothing's Impossible: Leadership Lessons From Inside And Outside The Classroom. US: PublicAffairs, 1999.

Robbins, Anthony. Unlimited Power. New, NY: Fawcett Columbine, 1986.

Seligman, Martin E. P. Learned Optimism: How to Change Your Mind and Your Life. US: Vintage, 2006.

Soultaris, Vangelis, and B.M. Marcello, Maestro. "The Case of Multitasking." Harvard Business Review 89 (October 2011): 32.

Stoltz, Paul G. Adversity Quotient: Turning Obstacles into Opportunities. US: Wiley, 1999.

Stoltz, Paul G. Adversity Quotient @ Work: Make Everyday Challenges the Key to Your Success – Putting the Principles of AQ Into Action. US: William Morrow, 2000.

Tabrizi, Behnam N. Rapid Transformation: A 90-day Plan for Fast and Effective Change. US: Harvard Business School Press, 2007.

Tannen, Deborah. Talking From 9 to 5: Women and Men in the Workplace: Language, Sex, and Power. New York, NY: William Morrow, and Company, 1994.

Thich Nhat Hanh. The Art of Power. US: HarperOne, 2008.

Tsu, Lao. Tao Te Ching. New York: Vintage Books, 2011.

Ury, William. Getting Past No. New York: Bantam, 1992.

Ury, William. The Power of a Positive No: Save The Deal Save The Relationship and Still Say No. New York: Bantam, 2007.

REALITY CHECK

"Only the Truth Sounds Like the Truth." Behar, Howard. It´s Not About the Coffee: Leadership Principles from a Life at Starbucks. US: Penguin Group, 2007.

Grimes, John. Reality Check. US: Ten Speed Press, 1993.

Grimes, John. Fuzzy logic: Cartoons. US: J. Grimes, 1998.

Kawasaki, Guy. Reality Check: The Irreverent Guide to Outsmarting, Outmanaging, and Outmarketing Your Competition. US: Portfolio Hardcover, 2008.

SYNC YOUR GEARS

Collins, Jim and Hansen, Morten, T. Great By Choice. US: HarperCollins books, 2011.

Mullins, John. The New Business Road Test: What entrepreneurs and executives should do before writing a business plan. US: FT Press, 2004.

MORE INSPIRATION

If you need more inspiration, please visit our website: **www.gearupventures.com.** If you are a company seeking more guidance on how the Gear Up model can help you, or if you would like to partner with us, please contact us.

PARTNERS USING THIS FRAMEWORK INCLUDE:

Stanford Center for Professional Development

Please contact Paul Marca for more information at pmarca@stanford.edu.

Stockholm School of Economics

Please contact Anders Richtnér for more information at anders.richtner@hhs.se.

Or contact **Gear Up Ventures**

Lena Ramfelt, one of the authors of this book, will help you find a good partner: lena@gearupventures.com.

NOTES

"BUSINESS IS SIMPLE. IN THE END
IT'S ALL ABOUT WINNING."

Continue your journey at
WWW.GEARUPVENTURES.COM